August '08

Dear Mark,

It was a pleasure to work with you. I hope we can play one of these courses in the future.
Thanks for your support,

Robbert.

Golf in the Tropics

Golf in the Tropics

Direction, design and editing / BENJAMÍN VILLEGAS

Production, research, and text / TUTE PUERTA

Photography / CRISTÓBAL VON ROTHKIRCH

Villegas
editores

Book desgined and edited in Colombia by
VILLEGAS ASOCIADOS S. A.
Avenida 82 No. 11-50, Interior 3
Bogotá, D. C., Colombia
Telephone (57-1) 616 1788
Fax (57-1) 616 0020
e-mail: informacion@VillegasEditores.com

© VILLEGAS EDITORES, 2003

Art Department
DAVID RENDÓN / OLGA LUCÍA NOVOA

English translation
MICHAEL KENNEDY

Proofreader
JIMMY WEISKOPF

Course map design
TUTE PUERTA

Course map graphics
HERNÁN HIGUERA / ARENA PRODUCTIONS

CONSULTANTS
MANUEL DE LA ROSA / Colombian Golf Federation President
JAIME RODRÍgUEZ / Colombian Golf Federation Secretary
CARLOS ROBERTO POMBO / Colombian PGA President
ROCÍo FONSECA / Colombia PGA Executive Director
DORIS ÁnGEL DE ECHEVERRI / Federation of Clubs President
FERNANDO GAMBOA
BORIS SOKOLOFF
RAFAEL VILLEGAS
JAIME VILLEGAS
PEDRO CárDENAS
CARLOS HOLGUÍn

Acknowledgements:

Juan Fernando Ramírez, Martín Arroyave, Carlos Andrés Velásquez, Jennifer Ponsford, Juan Pablo Gutiérrez, Álvaro Amaya, Luis Horacio Lotero, José María Rodríguez, Alejandro Pinilla, Rafael Amaya, Jaime Reyes, Roberto Herrera, Jorge Ángel, Santiago Jaramillo, Luis Guillermo Hoyos, José Quintero, Jorge Enrique Rodríguez, Jaime Ruiz, Gonzalo Silva, Fernando Ayala, José Antonio Martínez, Andrés Cabrera, Yolanda Rojas, Alejandro Castañeda, Jorge Alberto Mesa, Wilson Romero, Ernesto Samper, Fernando Paredes, Susie Faccini, Antonio Forero, Juan Pablo Coral Luna, Miguel Ángel Cuevas, Laurent Fosaert, Constanza Rodríguez, Carlos E. Montes, Cr. Carlos Ardila Dimat, Leonardo Contreras, Rosario Caro, Luis Fernando Serna, Martha Cecilia Jaramillo, Emilio Sardi, José Miguel Gómez, Humberto von Rothkirch, Francisco Torres, Lindon Rodríguez, Guillermo Vázquez, Ángel Wilder Ante, Carlos Rodríguez, Hernán Borrero, Luis Herrera, Alejandro Rodríguez, Jesús Asmed Osmar, Aldemar Balanta, Dora Inés Rojas, Jorge Elías Trujillo, Jorge Olmedo González, Arnulfo Ortiz, Alonso Valencia, Fernando Arango, Rubén Arango, Juan Cáceres, Mónica Escobar Rendón, César Gómez, María del Pilar Valencia, José Eddie Ortiz, Álvaro Pinedo, Libardo Ángel, Giomar González, Álvaro Zabala, Arley Ríos, Carlos Felipe Botero, Daniel Boada, Alberto Valenzuela, Luis Fernando Villegas, Alfonso Linares, Tito César Osorio, Francisco Soto, Juan Manuel Uribe, María Virginia Ocampo, Luis Jiménez, Jorge del Río, Alí Berrío Pitalúa, Lili Maldonado, Juan García, Lina María Pineda, Adriana Pineda, José Corredor, Julio Polonia, Rodolfo Azuero, Santiago Sanín, Carlos Idárraga, Camilo Obregón, Roberto Serna, Juan Diego Sánchez, Manuel José Arango, Juan Carlos Ledes, Rogelio González, Darío Obando, Germán Lehmann, Luis Ucrós.

The editor would like to thank Liliana Villegas for the initiative which led to the development and publication of this book; likewise, Lupi Herrera for the disinterested and generous cooperation that made this book possible.

First edition
November, 2003

ISBN
958-8156-33-5

Front jacket, Club Militar de Golf
Back jacket, Country Club Barranquilla
Page. 1, Club Campestre Popayán
Pages. 2-3, Club Campestre de Cali
Pages. 4-5, Club Payandé
Page. 6, Los Andes Golf Club / Club Los Arrayanes
Page.7, Club Militar de Golf
Page. 8, Country Club Bogotá
Page. 11, Los Lagartos
Page. 12, La Pradera de Potosí
Pages. 14-15, San Jacinto

CONTENT

GOLF: A PASSIONATE JOURNEY

Benjamín Villegas

Conjure up the wind, feel it electrify the atmosphere; feel the fire of the stroke and see the divot rise above the grass after a sharp hit; observe the water, lots of water, and notice a singular and indispensable ingredient: Passion. You will find all of this in a single swing at a golf ball. If it were possible to define golf in one word, this word would have to be "passion." The same passion that defines the creation of this book.

The satisfaction that derives from a good drive is felt at the instant of impact, extends through the trajectory of the ball and makes every muscle in the golfer's body tingle with pleasure. It is the same pleasure he feels when he correctly reads the direction of the wind, position of ball and lie of the grass; chooses the right club; and then sinks a birdie or an eagle.

When one speaks of golf, one speaks of a game governed by rules that may be applied to life itself: respect for one's surroundings, a disciplined conduct, honest competition and the inexplicable challenge of surpassing yourself. In few other human activities does respect for other people arise so naturally as in golf. It would be unthinkable not to leave a golf course in the pure state in which you found it. Everything on it is ruled by elementary rules of courtesy. Replacing the divot, treading lightly across the green, restoring the sand in the bunker for the next golfer – these and other norms form part of the unspoken protocol of this game, along with the respectful silence and stillness that your fellow golfers observe at the sacred moment of your swing. Like the celebrant of an ancient ritual, the golfer begins his preparation far from the field of combat: he carefully selects his outfit, checks his equipment, arranges his bag, chooses the balls and tees and other ceremonial artifacts he will use.

In Colombia, playing golf is an idyllic encounter with nature. To stroll around her courses is to enter into contact with a tropical environment that is hallucinatory and exotic. Surprisingly, however, up to now there was no book which spoke of these incomparable corners of our country, which described the beautiful features of these courses and the fascinating stories behind their construction and development. Filling this gap became an urgent – and pleasurable – obligation for me.

This book owes much to the professionalism of Tute Puerta, an unquestionable authority on golf, whose love for the game finds an ideal complement in the exquisite photos taken by the Colombian photographer Cristóbal von Rothkirch. As well as being a unique and indispensable work of reference, this book will give pleasure to golfers all over the world and show them the positive side of Colombia. We hope that this book will convey the excitement of playing golf in Colombia: the serenity of the skies that watch over its courses, the peculiarities of their greens, the holes which, whatever their difficulties, possess an inspiring beauty.

Club Campestre Hato Grande

INTRODUCTION

Tute Puerta

I wish to express my undying gratitude to my father, Fernando Puerta, for his dedication and self-surrender. He was, is and always will be the driving force behind my devotion to golf. The encouragement he gave me was such that I still feel his presence and lean on his strength. He taught me to love this country, to admire and appreciate it in all its grandeur. This work is dedicated to his memory.

The game of golf, as we know it today, was born in Scotland between the 14th and 15th centuries. Prohibited for a while in 1457, the ban was lifted by King James IV of Scotland, who authorized the playing of the game in the 16th century. His granddaughter, the famous Mary Stuart I, brought the game to France. The youth of the time who assisted the golfers were called "cadets", the word which gave origin to the term "caddy".

The history of golf architecture is defined by the changes which took place in equipment, course conditions and playing techniques. In broad terms, these fall into three epochs: that of the 19th century British links, the classical or "boom" period from 1900 to 1930, and the modern one, which began after the Second World War. "Links" is the name given to the seaside courses on which golf was invented. Their original architects were the natural forces of the tides, currents and winds that shaped their topography. The equipment and rules that arose were a response to the challenges they presented. The oldest link is the "Westward Ho!" course in northern Devon, in England. Up to 1700, approximately, either wooden balls were used or leather balls filled with wool or hair. The holes were much shorter than they are today and the average distance reached by a driver ranged between 150 and 180 yards. Until 1800 the clubs were almost always made of wood, while irons were only used sporadically.

In 1744 the "Gentlemen Golfers of Leith" wrote the first rules for the game of golf. In the 18th century the first golf associations were established. Among the earliest were "The Honorable Company of Edinburgh Golfers" (1744); the "St. Andrew Society of Golfers" (1754), renamed the "Royal and Ancient Golf Club of St. Andrews" in 1834; and the "Royal Blackheath" (1766). In North America the first association was the "Canada's Royal Montreal Golf Club" (1873). In 1888 the "St. Andrew's Golf Club of Yonkers," was founded in New York, the oldest still in existence in the U.S. In 1897 the "Royal & Ancient Club of St. Andrew's" established the rules that we follow today. Between 1900 and 1930 this sport expanded around the world and with this expansion traveled the classic architecture of golf courses. This period, known as the boom, coincided with the development of ball and club technology. Before the turn of the century, the gutta-percha ball (filled with a Malaysian tree gum) or "gutty" was replaced by the Haskell, which was used well into the 20th century. The gutty had replaced the leather ball and increased the average distance of a stroke by twenty to forty yards. The Haskell, made of elastic gums tightened around a core, provided a further forty to ninety yards of distance. By 1901 this ball had been adopted all over the world, following its success in the British and US Opens. At the close of this period these advances, together with those in golf club technology – steel shafts replaced hickory ones and the sand wedge was introduced – led course designers to redefine golf architecture.

Condominio Campestre El Peñón

The origins of golf in Colombia date back to 1915, when the game was played at La Magdalena course, in Bogotá, situated at what is now the downtown sector of 13th Avenue and 37th Street. On his return from one of his journeys to England, Don Joaquín Samper Brush brought not only the first proper sets of clubs, but also an enormous enthusiasm for the game, which he communicated to his friends, who joined with him to found The Bogotá Country Club in 1917.

In March of the following year, Carlos A. de Vengoechea adjudicated the first handicaps.

The first professionals to reach Colombia were two Englishmen, Thomas Tredell and Frank Appleby, who worked at The Bogotá Country Club in 1919. Afterwards many Argentines arrived, among them Miguel J. Sala and Alberto Serra.

At the end of 1945 a group of golfers from around the country met at the Hacienda San Joaquín – now known as the Cali Country Club – and founded the Golfers Association ("Asogolf"), which is known today as the Colombian Federation of Golf.

During the 1950's, Alberto Serra helped to train the first Colombian professionals. In 1956, these professionals, headed by Miguel J. Sala , created the "Professional Golfers Association" (PGA) in Colombia.

After World War II, Robert Trent Jones´ redesign of Oakland Hills for the 1951 US Open initiated what is now called modern golf architecture. In order to meet the needs of this new architecture, bulldozers and cranes replaced mules and spades.

This new technology gave golf course architects the opportunity to adapt the terrain to their own theories of design: to give way to the temptation of radical transformation in order to create the most fantastic – or awe-inspiring – holes.

In general terms, the majority of golf courses in Colombia follow the classic canons. The transition from classic to modern design is best seen, perhaps, at courses like El Peñón and Peñalisa. The courses which definitively show the imprint of modern design are those of Ruitoque, Payandé, La Pradera, San Jacinto, Guaymaral 2 and Mesa de Yeguas.

In golf, three broad schools of thought govern the design of courses: there is the school of penalty or punishment, the heroic one and the strategic. All of these tendencies may be seen in the design of the courses that are found in Colombia.

In the penalty school of golf design, hazards are placed from the tee to the green in order to punish a poorly played shot. However, there are also holes which are theoretically chastising but nevertheless reward a good shot. One example is the second hole at the Pereira Country Club, where the many hazards, outs and slopes penalize the slightest error. To play this hole, you must place the ball very well, often sacrificing distance to correct placement.

From the onset of the golden age of golf at the beginning of the 20th century, the strategic school became the preferred design Here, the essential feature are greens staunchly defended by bunkers, lakes or sloping ground on one side. You gain

the advantage by placing the ball on a safe part of the fairway. The purpose of the hazards is to establish the optimum lines of attack of a dangerous green. This is the most widely followed school in Colombian courses. In the heroic school one has the opportunity to secure an advantage by a clear frontal attack from the tee. The ideal heroic hazard is an oblique one, so that all players are allowed an opportunity to choose the degree of risk, according to the conditions of the hole and their respective abilities. The fourth at Club Hato Grande, a par 4, is a good example of this school. A lake which runs from the tee to the green, gradually encroaching on the fairway from the left, offers players the possibility of deciding how bold they want to be.

Both the heroic and strategic schools oblige the golfer to weigh the risk he will take against the advantage he will obtain for the following shot to the green. His attack must be based on an honest evaluation of his talents.

An alternative concept is to reward the player not only for achieving a straight, long shot, but also for his ability to control its flight with his swing technique.

A handicap is the advantage, with regard to par, that the golfer is awarded on the basis of his skill at the game. To establish a uniform standard for players on different courses, the United States Golf Association (USGA), employs two criteria: the performance of the scratch (low handicap) player on the course, which is compared to that of the bogey (high handicap) player. The difficulty of the course itself is evaluated in terms of its topography, roll, greens, wind, fairways, roughs, bunkers, outs and hazards, on a scale of one to ten.

The USGA has authorized the Colombian Federation of Golf to employ the same system for Colombian courses.

As well as being a sport that is open to all, encouraging and stimulating interpersonal relations, golf is an activity which benefits the environment. It beautifies our surroundings, both in aesthetic and urbanistic terms through reforestation of the terrain, the conservation of native vegetation and the protection of the natural habit of fauna and flora. In many cases, the irrigation systems golf courses employ represent a pioneering effort to reutilize waste waters.

Nevertheless, given the natural blessings of the country in which they are found, Colombian courses do not have to interfere much with the landscape in order to protect nature: they mostly rely on and exalt the exuberant natural features that have always been an integral part of their respective regions. Taking advantage of the country's privileged geographical position, its wide range of climate and topography, the astonishing diversity of its fauna and vegetation, our golf courses manage to combine technical challenges with the natural magic of their emplacements.

Club Campestre Guaymaral
Page. 24, *Club Campestre Guaymaral*
Page. 25, *Club Payandé*

COLOMBIA

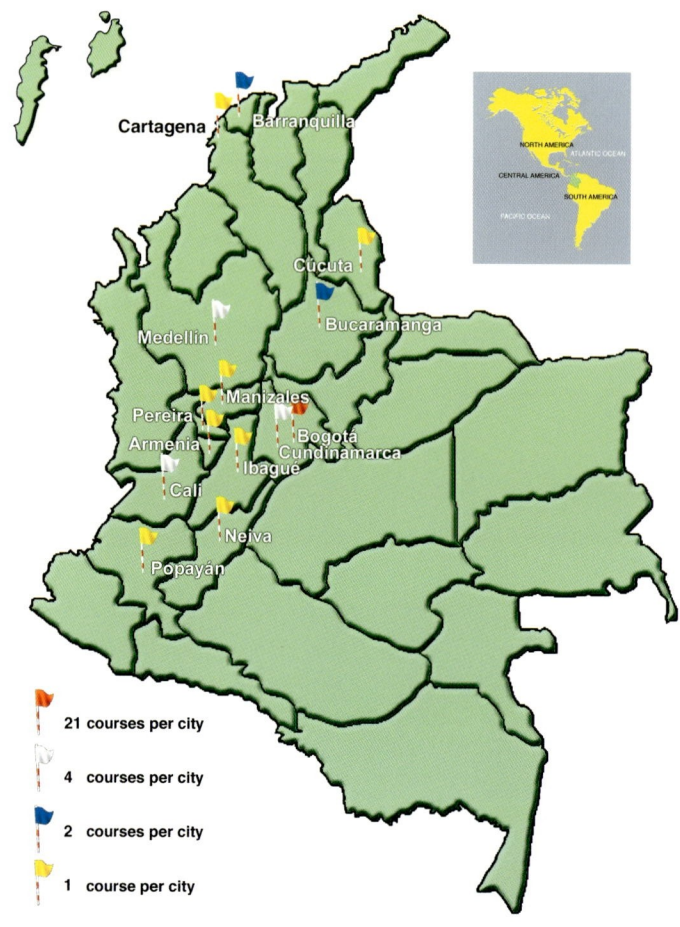

To play golf in Colombia is to experience the interplay of the basic elements of life: earth, wind, water and fire. As the editor points out in the introduction to this book, golf and the courses it is played on celebrate these elements and invite the golfer to undertake a passionate journey. Along the cordilleras of the Andes the element of earth finds its maximum expression. Here, in Colombia, the highly varied topography that gives rise to its majestic mountains includes rain forests, prairies, the high Andean moors known as paramos, and areas of perpetual snow. Colombia boasts of all the thermal levels found in Nature and their different climates and ecosystems are responsible for its amazing variety of vegetation. These factors – altitude, climate and vegetation – play a critical role in the design of its golf courses and the demands of the game that is played on them. Wind is a decisive element as well. The trade winds from the poles, together with those that circulate locally, determine the times when the dry and rainy seasons occur in Colombia. At times, the ball struggles against the wind. At times, it takes advantage of it to reach the green and the flag… or suffer the penalty of being driven into a sand trap or a water hazard. As for water, well, it is practically synonymous with a country which is the world's second richest in hydraulic resources. You find it everywhere and it influences the way that golf is played here as in no other place on the planet. Rivers, lakes, lagoons and marshes irrigate, run through and embellish all of the courses of Colombia. The country also boasts of nearly 3000 kilometers of coastline along two oceans – the Atlantic and Pacific – as well as an impressive number of islands.

And, as in few other countries, fire is a dominant element in Colombia, with its forty-five volcanoes and variety of mineral resources: it is the world's biggest producer of top-quality emeralds and possesses rich reserves of petroleum, coal, natural gas, gold, iron, salt, and platinum. Most precious, however, are her forty million inhabitants, their racial diversity and the country's extraordinary cultural wealth. The diversity of her flora and fauna matches her geographical and cultural variety. Considered to have the world's highest per hectare biodiversity in plants, Colombia has an immeasurable number of species of flora. So great is the natural wealth of the country that it can only be measured and understood by dividing it into regions, the same regions which influence the topography of its golf courses and form the basis for the arrangement of this book, which follows the regional divisions authorized by the Colombian Federation of Golf.

Although there are, in different parts of the country, ten high-level executive courses and numerous practice ranges, courses that we present in this book for the delight of our readers have one trait in common. They are fully equipped to host professional golf tournaments and for that reason, are perfect places to experience the passion of golf in body and soul.

Farallones Club Campestre
Page. 28, *San Andrés Golf Club /*
Carmel Club Campestre
Page. 29, *Los Lagartos*

CENTRAL ZONE

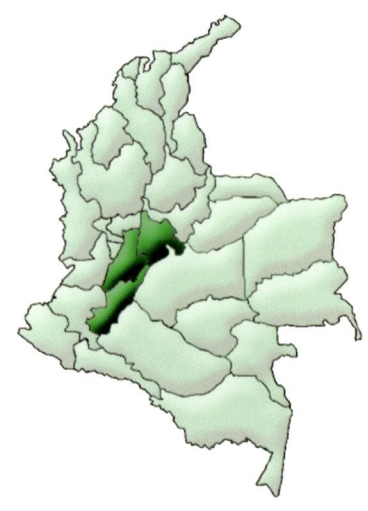

This sector is filled with rivers, tributaries and streams, flanked by the immense mountain ranges from which descends the Magdalena River – the great fluvial artery of the country that often crosses Colombia's golf courses. In this zone, the dry months include January, February, June, July, August and December.

To the south the towns of San Agustín and Tierradentro are the Mecca of archaelogical tourism in Colombia. In Tierradentro exist remains of the great pre-Colombian cultures that flourished there before the Aztecs and Incas, a collection of ruins and relics that are known to and proclaimed by the international scientific community. In 1995, San Agustín was declared by the Unesco to form part of the historical and cultural "Patrimony of Mankind". Its mysterious pre-Colombian societies left a wealth of stone statuary, including burial sites with monolithic sarcophagi and rock statues of human-beast images that reflect the culture's magical-religious beliefs about death and the afterlife.

Continuing south one encounters Neiva, a place rich in folkloric dances and songs and the site of Colombia's festival of "bambuco" music. Further on, along the banks of the river Combeima, you will reach Ibagué, known as the musical city of Colombia. Not very far from there lie Villeta, Melgar, Anapoima and Giradot, holiday spots for people from Bogotá because of their sunny weather. In this same region one can find the "Desert of the Tatacoa," which is celebrated for its large number of well-preserved fossils and strange landscape. The dam of Betania, the greatest in the country, and another on the Prado River, are places apt for aquatic sports. In Rivera you can enjoy bathing in the hot springs and there is river rafting on the nearby Tobia River. The "Caja de Agua," is an enormous cavern with a waterfall which cascades from a height of thirty meters and curtains the entrance. This passage takes one to a national park reserve – the "Cueva de los Guácharos – with its impressive natural caverns and fountains.

The harsh climate and rugged features of the high Andes – the deep canyons, ancient glacial valleys and abundant lagoons of the "Nevado del Huila" national park – constitute another attraction of the region. In this zone the chromatic range of the vegetation is unimaginable, and the weather changes as much as the terrain. There, especially in the mornings, the heat of the desert mixes with the cold air from the mountains and sometimes blankets golf players in fog.

"Character" is perhaps the best word to define the special quality of the zone's golf courses. They are as joyful as the "sanjuanero" music played at the region's festivals but as difficult to read as the enigmatic sanctuaries of San Agustín or Tierradentro.Its golf courses will inevitably leave a deep mark on your heart and find a special place in your memory.

Puerto Peñalisa

MESA DE YEGUAS COUNTRY CLUB

Address: Vereda El Cabral, Anapoima
Altitude: 689 meter above sea level
Average temperature: 25 °C
Yards: 3614
Holes: 9, par-36
Designer: Robert Trent Jones, Jr.
(At the present time, only holes 10-18 are finished)
Bogotá population: 6 700 000

This is a set of private residences built around a golf course, rather than a golf course built into a residential area; the course is not compromised in any way with regard to the specifications of the USGA. The golfer here is assured of an excellent sporting challenge.

The eleventh is the most beautiful hole and the most dramatic, a par-4, measuring 466 yards; it tees off at forty-six meters above the fairway. This fairway, whose entrance is protected by a gigantic *samán* tree, is forty-five yards wide, uneven and has outs on both sides. The floating green is wide and is guarded by a bunker to the left.

The tees are planted in Bermuda 419. Each hole has between four to six tees in different places and geared to different distances, which change the characteristics of the hole according to the placement of the marks.

The fairways are planted in Bermuda 419 and 422: their width varies from forty to eighty yards, and they are very uneven, offering terraces that provide different approaches to play for those who attack the course or for those whose play is conservative.

The special characteristic of this course are the bunkers found in the design: from the tee one can see all the bunkers; however, from the green to the tee the same bunkers are not always visible.

The roughs have two classes of grass. Next to the fairway, the Bermuda 419 is cut higher; in other places it combines with native grasses, angleton and penisetum, characterized by a long and thin leaf that looks like wheat.

The ornamental lakes, adorned by large stones and surrounded by aquatic gardens, make it a particularly beautiful sight; however, the majority of the greens are elevated and unadorned by vegetation. They stand alone, are uneven and planted in tifton dwarf: they measure 640 square meters. They are a remarkable sight from a distance, where they appear to float amidst the mountains that rise up all around them.

Along the course one finds many hundreds of *samán*, *orejero*, *pata de vaca*, acacia and *caracolí* trees. In this zone live armadillos and anteaters; likewise, one can see at least 120 of the 1700 species of birds that live in Colombia, such as royal egrets, snow egrets, striped egrets, fisher eagles, ducks, *toches*, *sangretoros*, *turpiales*, *guacharacas*, hummingbirds, *sinsontes* and *semilleros*. The assembly of these birds pays homage to nature. Here the ritual of golfing takes place in an atmosphere of sacred and respectful harmony that becomes a true song of life.

HOLE	PAR	▨	▨	▢	▨	HOLE	PAR	▨	▨	▢	▨
1	4	450	425	390	350	10	5	561	541	511	472
2	5	560	530	505	465	11	4	466	446	428	356
3	3	160	125	110	95	12	3	243	211	171	137
4	4	405	365	325	2957	13	4	385	366	331	291
5	4	445	420	390	360	14	3	159	141	135	120
6	3	170	135	125	95	15	5	599	575	546	490
7	5	525	490	450	4202	16	4	345	325	309	237
8	4	350	310	290	270	17	4	421	395	373	319
9	4	450	420	390	345	18	4	435	405	379	350
IN	36	3515	3220	2975	2695	OUT	36	3614	3405	3183	2772
						TOTAL	72	7129	6625	6158	5467

CLUB PAYANDÉ

Address: La Vega-Villeta Road, town of Quebradanegra
Altitude: 900 meters above sea level
Average temperature: 22-28 °C
Yards: 7012
Holes: 18, par-72
Designer: Scott Miller (1997)
Bogotá population: 6 700 000

"Very few golf courses can be described in a single word but when the land, the club and the golf course are the best of the best, like Payandé, the word ´pure´ says everything." That is what Scott Miller, its designer, said about this course in a note that he wrote for this book. And who better than he to speak about golf course design?

About the design process he notes: "The site selected for this golf course had all of the best characteristics for the building of a first-rate, world-class course; there was more than sufficient space, including rich alluvial earth alongside the beautiful River Tobia, an area known for its excellent climate and lush vegetation. The railroad that crosses the course forms a historical link with those marvelous Irish and Scottish ones where railway lines cut across the fairways. The eighteenth is a classic, heroic hole. One excellent drive will give the golfer a chance to land on the green in only two strokes on this par-5. A precise stroke will result in an eagle or a birdie. However, a poor shot will land in disaster. Each golfer must decide how to attack this hole before getting to the green, based on an honest assessment of his talent and experience. This is a great hole to end on, as it offers many options and is rather dramatic." Later, he mentioned, "I believe that golf courses, much like people, are frequently dealt with on the basis of a first impression; thus, I designed the tees of holes one and ten by taking advantage of the nearly twenty meters elevation to provide them with certain dramatic effect at the entrance." About the course´s first sketch, Miller says, "The course was designed with the aim of giving the golfer an opportunity to score well within the first seven holes. Holes eight to thirteen were designed so that he would be able to recuperate his game and improve his score. In the final part of the course there are a series of very exciting high-risk reward-penalty holes."

The golf courses that were designed by Miller have at least one short par-4. "The sixteenth offers a good example. This hole offers the average golfer a realistic chance to get a par or a birdie, and build up his confidence for the last two holes of the course, which are the most challenging. The low-handicap golfer counts upon making a birdie in this hole; if not, his frustration may lead him to get bogeys in the last holes."

On this course, whose name is inspired by the surrounding native trees, the water-sprinkling system is automatic. The grass of both the tees and fairways is Bermuda 419, whereas the grass of the roughs is *Bahía Argentina*, while the greens are tifton dwarf. According to Miller, "Payandé requires a perfect game and therefore inspires long drives with the irons and the ability to read the wind and play the ball accordingly. Perhaps the key thing to regard the greens of this course as one regards a work of art: the best results come when you make yourself familiar with the minutest details."

HOLE	PAR	■	■	□	■	HOLE	PAR	■	■	□	■
1	4	447	432	329	270	10	4	464	442	350	257
2	5	484	455	429	387	11	5	624	526	519	490
3	4	425	382	360	337	12	3	155	143	131	84
4	4	433	393	379	302	13	4	462	431	373	304
5	3	176	153	135	90	14	4	393	372	312	254
6	4	251	232	202	186	15	3	185	150	133	97
7	5	553	536	472	407	16	4	302	242	234	215
8	3	219	201	180	128	17	4	446	435	397	336
9	4	481	437	409	301	18	5	539	485	464	384
IN	**36**	**3469**	**3221**	**2895**	**2408**	**OUT**	**36**	**3569**	**3226**	**2913**	**2421**
						TOTAL	**72**	**7038**	**6447**	**5808**	**4829**

PUERTO PEÑALISA

Adress: Melgar-Girardot Road, km 5
Altitude: 1185 meters above sea level
Average temperature: 34 °C
Yards: 6838
Holes: 18, par-72
Designer: Gary Player Design Co. Constructor Boris Sokoloff (1995)
Bogotá population: 6 700 00

The surrounding homes and buildings respect and harmonize with the course and set off its beautiful design. The design is quite varied and takes advantage of the uneven terrain, particularly during the second round. One needs to prepare a good strategy for this course, especially when facing the tee off. If you are a powerful driver, you will inevitably find that certain holes are alluring and will not be able to resist a full frontal attack, regardless of their respective hazards, outs, and places where trees are strategically placed to interfere with the golfer's game.

The fifteenth, a par-4 of 410 yards, allows the golfer to enjoy the stupendous surroundings. In the area just before the tee one can see the lake bordered by majestic mountains. One rubber tree, which stands right in the middle of the fairway, at a distance of 240 yards from the tee, marks a reference point. From there the fairway begins to descend and continues until it reaches the lake. At the rear edge of the green stand a group of *achiote* trees that accentuate the backdrop. At the entrance to the green there is a very deep bunker and at the back you find three more - not as menacingly deep – as well as the lake.

The tees, planted in Bermuda grass 419, are circular; some of them are elevated, and the others stand at course level. Each mark is placed in a different location and offers a different angle from which to launch a drive. The ample fairways are approximately 60-70 yards wide. They are level in the outward nine and more or less uneven during the inward one. The roughs are planted in Bermuda grass mixed with native grasses. When the course's level of difficulty needs to be increased, the administration cuts the grass higher, which packs the grass and leaves it heavier and more resistant.

Puerto Peñalisa has twenty-six very deep bunkers and in most cases, they serve to protect the players from the frequent risk of landing in water. There are three grass bunkers and a few cross-bunkers. The sand is gray, thick, granular, and loose. The Sumapaz River and rainwater overflow into a canal that feeds the five lakes of Puerto Peñalisa's golf course.

The run ups to the greens are cut so as to maintain the same level as the fairways. They are a bit long and often trap the ball and force the golfer to use middle irons and of course execute precise shots deftly. The greens are level and measure on average 750 square meters; they are planted in Bermuda grass 328.

In Puerto Peñalisa one may find a variety of fauna, especially little animals like iguanas and caimans, and, among the birds, canaries, macaws and wood ducks. The diverse vegetation characteristic of this course includes coconut palms, fan palms and balsams. Variety is the only constant feature of this exquisite course, where, at every turn, golfing takes place in natural surroundings that inspire moments of ecstasy and contemplation.

HOLE	PAR	HAND	🟦	⬜	🟥	HOLE	PAR	HAND	🟦	⬜	🟥
1	5	2	545	520	440	10	5	1	548	517	435
2	4	12	411	386	305	11	3	17	175	140	100
3	3	18	185	155	133	12	4	13	386	343	269
4	4	14	378	348	265	13	4	9	393	365	290
5	4	8	393	364	293	14	4	3	422	382	307
6	5	4	551	510	439	15	4	5	410	387	312
7	4	6	407	375	299	16	4	15	344	317	244
8	3	16	175	153	148	17	3	11	209	184	133
9	4	10	377	335	267	18	5	7	529	508	418
IN	**36**		**3422**	**3146**	**2589**	**OUT**	**36**		**3416**	**3143**	**2508**
						TOTAL	**72**		**6838**	**6289**	**5097**

RATING (NORMAL)	72.8	70.0	69.7

CLUB CAMPESTRE DE NEIVA

Address: Highway to the South, km 12, Neiva
Altitude: 442 meters above sea level
Average temperature: 28 °C
Yards: 6505
Holes: 18, par-72
Designer: Fernando Gamboa (1987)
Neiva population: 350 000

This golf course alongside the Magdalena River is divided into two parts: the river holes and the older holes. The old part is classically designed, with level, narrow fairways lined by trees and small, slow and level greens. The river holes weave their way through a group of single-family residences and are marked by many outs: their fairways are also much wider and less level and feature many lakes and bunkers to protect their greens. This golf course demands great precision from the beginning, and one error forces the golfer to face the danger of many following ones; the golfer frequently learns to sacrifice a shot to the center of the fairway or the run up to the green. At the old holes, if your drive to the green fails, you can recuperate with the following approach shot. Here, the run ups to the greens are less difficult and the greens themselves are noticeably more level and easier to read. On the river holes, by contrast, one needs to carefully finesse shots on the ante greens and at places where the terrain is more uneven. The bunkers have firm, compacted sand and the greens have hollows that are difficult to decipher.

The third, a par-4 of 497 yards, is very long and straight. It is so complicated that the local golfers call this hole "catrasca," a term difficult to translate but easy to understand: it simply means that when a golfer fails a drive the ball will fall into a series of problems that only lead to other difficulties. With the out to the left, the course is adorned by five lakes that are beautiful but insidious, presenting a lot of difficulties along this part in particular: one lake next to the tee, three others to the right – preceded by a cross bunker – and another lake at the level of the green. The green has a bunker at the back and to the left.

The hole requires the golfer to play the ball with precision and go for distance from the very start. For the second shot one must hit the ball exactly: if not, the golfer will not be able to reach the green: the ball will probably go out, or wind up in the lake or the bunker. Tees four and fifteen converge at a spot that is considered to be the most breathtaking place on the course. From there one cannot help admiring the panorama.

The tees are rectangular, high, and planted in Bermuda 419, as are the roughs and fairways, all of which are narrow and adapted to the natural level of the terrain. The greens are tough and flat and planted in Bermuda grass 328. In the older holes above all, the difficulty of the rough is compounded by the stands of trees that are found there. On the riverside, between the fairways and the out, the fairways are lined by trees that narrow their width. Twenty-one lakes, most of which are small, provide the player with front and lateral hazards. There are forty-six bunkers consisting of a rather heavy, gray, compact and firm river sand. On this course the lush tropics are seen in all their glory. So, enjoy the beautiful scenery, but… beware!

HOLE	PAR	HAND	🟦	⬜	🟥	HOLE	PAR	HAND	🟦	⬜	🟥
1	4	13	440	370	310	10	5	2	520	512	434
2	3	3	167	150	110	11	5	8	509	497	447
3	4	17	480	430	365	12	3	14	164	152	140
4	5	9	497	486	426	13	4	18	265	249	235
5	5	7	560	503	443	14	5	12	504	490	440
6	3	11	195	181	171	15	3	10	205	188	172
7	4	5	325	310	300	16	4	6	310	298	286
8	4	15	380	360	340	17	3	16	139	129	120
9	4	1	430	417	367	18	4	4	415	400	386
IN	36		3474	3207	2832	OUT	36		3031	2915	2610
						TOTAL	72		6505	6122	5442

RATING	🟦	⬜	🟥
	71.1	72.2	74.2

CONDOMINIO CAMPESTRE EL PEÑÓN

Address: Vereda Portachuelo. Girardot
Altitude: 315 meters above sea level
Average temperature: 25-28 °C
Yards: 7020
Holess: 18, par-72
Designer: Charles Mark Mahannah Co. and Rafael López Uribe & Cía. Ltda. (1978)
Bogotá population: 6 700 000

The terrain alongside the Bogotá River, which is shared by private homes, presents many challenges. To play here one has to be prepared for a long course with wide and uneven fairways. Here on this course the golfer has to face not only certain inherent technical difficulties, but also the wet and often very hot weather.

The tenth, a par-4 of 340 yards, is one of the most beautiful and difficult holes on this course; it demands a lot of scrutiny and precision from the beginning. To the left an immense lake surrounded by palm trees awaits the player, and if he slices the ball, he will probably land in the rough lined with trees, an out that might complicate the following shot. Two large bunkers to the right, in the landing area, and the slightly undulating fairway require all of your attention when you drive for the green. The green is protected by two imposing sentinels, large and deep bunkers on either side, and stands a bit higher than the fairway. Its nearly imperceptible falls and grass traps make it very deceptive.

The eighteenth, a par-5 of 555 yards, offers a continuous out along both sides of the course. The fairway tilts severely from right to left. The first drive must be powerful and straight. To the left side there is the out, and to the right resides a bunker; the lakes and trees leave little space when you try to keep the ball in the center of the fairway. The second shot is dramatic too, at this distance of the fairway, as the ball tends to jump towards the out. The golfer should strive to keep the ball on the right side in order to avoid the bunker to the left. The shot to the green is much better played on the right, as it has a great slope tilting down to the left.

The tees are rectangular platforms planted in the same Bermuda grass as the wide fairways, which, where they are not naturally uneven, have been made so by the designer. It is a highly challenging course, mostly because of its highly varied topography. The trees, especially the *ficus*, easily intercept the ball and represent the major difficulty of the roughs. The *ficus* trees are accompanied by coconut palms, acacias, eucalyptuses and fruit trees like lemon, orange, and mango.

The seventy-six bunkers, all with loose, thick sand, are rather deep in the majority of cases and require a great deal of precision and finesse. The greens measure 450 square meters: they are planted in Bermuda 328 and demand caution, as they are uneven and heavy. Along the course are thirteen lakes, which shape the terrain surrounding the next thirteen holes; the Bogotá River crosses to the left of holes fourteen, seventeen and eighteen. Iguanas, caimans, lizards, squirrels, and foxes constantly scamper across the course. The tough challenges, constant surprises and surrounding views make any game on this course a marvelous experience.

HOLE	PAR	HAND	🟦	⬜	🟥	HOLE	PAR	HAND	🟦	⬜	🟥
1	5	2	545	515	485	10	4	3	430	405	382
2	3	18	180	175	132	11	3	17	200	180	150
3	4	12	390	386	320	12	5	9	540	495	439
4	4	14	430	426	356	13	3	15	215	195	151
5	4	10	415	400	325	14	4	5	420	413	370
6	4	6	395	390	330	15	4	11	410	404	347
7	4	8	400	380	338	16	5	7	525	472	437
8	3	16	200	195	157	17	3	13	235	200	166
9	5	4	535	530	491	18	5	1	555	515	404
IN	**36**		**3490**	**3397**	**2934**	**OUT**	**36**		**3530**	**3279**	**2846**
						TOTAL	**72**		**7020**	**6676**	**5780**
						RATING			**74.1**	**72.2**	**73.3**

CLUB CAMPESTRE DE IBAGUÉ

Address: Picaleña-Ibagué Road, km 7
Altitude: 1248 meters above sea level
Average temperature: 21 °C
Yards: 6516
Holes: 18, par-71
Designer: Fernando Gamboa (1987)
Ibagué population: 435 000

The Combeima River feeds the five lakes that are connected to one another by canals, which cross eleven of the 18 holes. This course has narrow fairways; the tees and greens are difficult. The designer took great advantage of the naturally hilly, clay- and rock-filled terrain when pondering the design of this course. The spongy greens are difficult to land on; therefore, the challenge of placing the ball on the green requires great finesse. There are many trees that constantly interfere with the golfer's game and the roughs are heavy.

The eighteenth, a par-5 of 514 yards, is interesting because of an out that stretches 344 yards along the fairway; between the 170 and 230 yards markers the fairway is crossed by four channels of water separated by a high, dense rough. If you are not the timid sort, and want to run the risk with a driver, with finesse and luck you'll land beyond the channels. Playing in this way, the opportunity to reach the green in two is yours. Another way to play this shot would be to place the ball as close to the channels as possible, in order to carefully carry out the strategy for the next shot, which requires you to keep in mind the three cross-bunkers that lie to the left, between 260 and 300 yards. At this point the fairway bends to the left and climbs to the green, which is protected by a bunker in the middle, 50 yards before the green, and two more that stand on either side.

The tees, planted in Bermuda 419, generally have two levels, which separate the long marks from the others. The fairways are narrow and planted, like the tees, in Bermuda 419. The roughs are planted in *trenza* grass.

The greens are slightly elevated and measure 500 square meters. They are level and at the back are planted, additionally, in tifton dwarf and Bermuda 328; of course, they do not easily hold the ball and the challenge is compounded by the 42 bunkers that protect them. The bunkers are filled with a silty powder of the finest river sand.

Pink and red *ocobos*, *tulipanes*, *ficus*, *araucarias*, *pera de maloca*, *crotos*, *jacarandas*, *gualandayes*, *samanes*, palms, *tachuelos*, *cachimbos*, acacias, *guásimos*, *matarratones*, and *caracolíes* are some of the timber trees that you will see on this course. There are such fruit trees as mango, *mamoncillo*, guava, orange, lemon, mandarin, *pomarrosa* and *guamo*.

Among the birds that visit it are white and black egrets, mallards, woodpeckers, cardinals and canaries. And the animals include foxes, iguanas and wolves, which appear on or around the course at different times of the year.

Surrounded by a spacious terrain of mountains, the setting of this course offers the golfer the perfect place to practice many different types of swings and shots. Above all, it is a course that requires great precision and finesse in every shot – especially from the tees.

HOLE	PAR	HAND	🟦	⬜	🟥	HOLE	PAR	HAND	🟦	⬜	🟥
1	4	7	378	367	325	10	4	14	350	337	350
2	3	11	204	169	335	11	3	10	208	195	420
3	4	13	405	394	140	12	4	12	376	358	305
4	5	5	507	483	383	13	4	4	396	385	110
5	4	3	426	415	300	14	3	8	205	194	290
6	4	15	364	352	310	15	4	6	393	386	300
7	5	1	502	484	393	16	4	18	364	352	270
8	3	17	159	155	135	17	4	16	385	373	145
9	4	9	380	368	300	18	5	2	514	483	472
IN	36		3325	3187	3591	OUT	35		3191	3052	2698
						TOTAL	71		6516	6239	5605

RATING (NORMAL)	70.0	68.9	71.1
RATING (WIND)	71.8	70.6	71.9

MEDELLÍN ZONE

Situated in the narrow Aburrá Valley and surrounded by high mountains, the city of Medellín runs from south to north and is bifurcated by the river that gives it its name.. This is the capital of the Department of Antioquia, whose inhabitants are known as "Paisas": they have a reputation for being adventurous dreamers who nevertheless possess a sound business sense. The men who explored and opened up this mountainous region dedicated themselves to the mining and commercialization of precious metals and minerals. Arriving on mule back to establish the first settlements, they were driven by a disciplined work ethic, a pragmatic approach to business deals and an austere lifestyle.

Blessed by an ideal climate, Medellín is one of the major centers of commerce in Colombia. A leader in the design and manufacture of clothing, the city boasts of the most important textile factory in South America. In addition to precious gems and metals, the region produces coffee, bananas and flowers, among other important export products. Medellín has a reputation for offering excellent services in health care due to its advanced technology and medical research, especially in the field of organ transplants. Impressive malls are found throughout the city and outlying region. Possessor of a rich musical, theatrical, and visual arts tradition, the city has museums that are a must for all tourists. Fernando Botero, the great Colombian painter and sculptor, was born in this proud capital and has donated some of his most important pieces to the city.

The city encourages an open-minded attitude towards all sorts of business opportunities but deal-making is pleasantly combined with the boundless hospitality and genuine warmth of its inhabitants Its cuisine is known throughout the country and is a key feature of the Paisa identity.

Views of the surrounding mountains, a hilly topography, forests of gigantic trees with lush vegetation and a climate of perpetual Spring make its golf courses an inevitable meeting place for the business community, a place to meet friends and talk over deals, while enjoying the natural surroundings.

On the four courses in this zone you will enjoy the diversity and spirit of this generous land. On the Rodeo golf course you must learn how to negotiate the many challenges of a demanding round: don't forget to prepare your strategy! At the Macarena you will learn something about the difficult terrain that made the journeys of the first explorers of these mountains so arduous. At Llano Grande you will experience a delight akin to that of the local musicians who play the "*tiple*," a typical guitar of the region, which whispers and seduces with a type of music known here as the "*Bambuco*." At Campestre you will feel the drive to succeed and joy of life that are so typical of the *Paisa* .

Club Campestre El Rodeo

CLUB CAMPESTRE EL RODEO
Medellín

Address: 2nd Street south # 65- 535
Altitude: 1486 meters above sea level
Average temperature: 24 ºC
Yards: 6808
Holes: 18, par-72
Designer: Canadian Golf Landscaping (1954)
Medellín population: 2 026 000

Built on the flanks of a great mountain, this course undulates dramatically: many of her holes take full advantage of the natural slopes of this terrain. Due to this layout, it is rare that the golfer will find the ball resting on his own level after making a shot: it will wind up either above or below his feet.

The fourth, a par-5 of 510 yards, is a good example of the general characteristics of this golf course. For the first sixty or seventy yards the fairway is tight and is surrounded by very tall trees; therefore, it demands a straight and long hit at the start. At 160 yards from the tee, the fairway begins to descend, which means that it is practically impossible to know where the ball will fall at the end of its flight. At approximately 280 yards the course detours to the left and the fairway begins to climb again. If you have a good first stroke and the ball lands in a good place, it is possible to reach the green in two shots and get either a birdie or an eagle. On the other hand, you must take into account that, because of the sloping fairway, this is a blind shot and has to cross over the hill that hides the green from you. Play the shot to the right side so that the ball will land on and run down the far side of the hill and thus take maximum advantage of the available natural momentum: you will then face only one shot down to the green. Remember that two deep bunkers protect the green, one guarding the entrance and the other sitting to the right. The run up to the green is raised above the level of the green itself, making the approach even more interesting and presenting a definite challenge.

The tees are planted in Bermuda 328, have a traditional design and are elevated above the level of the fairways; some holes have a clear view, whereas in others the shot from the tees is blind. The fairways, planted in the same grass, undulate and incline; they are narrow at the tees but quickly widen, at fifty or sixty yards. The greens, some planted in Bermuda 328 and others planted in tifton dwarf, are uneven and measure 400 square meters: these greens are protected by well-placed bunkers.

The little Guayabala River feeds the course and its six lakes. In the roughs one finds a combination of grasses, Colombian *macana*, *trenza* and bay grass, among them. One will also find ornamental trees like *urapanes*, *cascos de vaca*, cypresses and palms. The surroundings of this golf course are a combination of the natural and the manmade, the latter giving it one peculiarity: from the second and seventeenth holes one can see the runways of the Olaya Herrera Airport. The airplanes fly so close that at times one has the sensation that they may land on the green of the seventeenth hole. To the right of these holes is situated a cemetery, an ironic contrast with the sense of life expressed by the game of golf.

HOLE	PAR	HAND Men	HAND Women	🟦	⬜	🔺	🟥	HOLE	PAR	HAND Men	HAND Women	🟦	⬜	🔺	🟥
1	4	5	7	417	405	361	332	10	4	14	12	333	325	310	306
2	3	17	17	165	160	150	125	11	5	2	4	530	501	491	432
3	4	9	9	380	370	360	340	12	4	6	8	411	388	317	296
4	5	3	3	510	500	490	466	13	4	8	10	415	344	340	310
5	4	13	13	400	390	380	324	14	5	4	2	470	460	420	416
6	4	11	11	365	355	345	316	15	3	18	16	216	199	185	180
7	5	1	1	513	507	497	448	16	3	16	18	210	190	155	153
8	3	15	15	208	198	165	147	17	4	10	14	455	430	395	346
9	4	7	5	420	410	400	341	18	4	12	6	390	380	370	326
IN	36			3378	3296	3148	2839	OUT	36			3430	3217	2983	2765
								TOTAL	72			6808	6612	6131	5604

	RATING	71.7	70.3	73.6	70.7

CORPORACIÓN CLUB CAMPESTRE DE MEDELLÍN
Llano Grande course

Address: Vereda Cabeceras, Rionegro
Altitude: 2150 meters above sea level
Average temperature: 17 °C
Yards: 7022
Holes: 18, par-72
Designer: Jaime and Rafael Villegas (1987)
Medellín population: 2 026 000

If you plan to play on this golf course, you must be prepared for a long, level, yet misleading course. Being very open, this golf course offers short cuts at some holes, where the ball can be played across neighboring fairways. The bunkers are not so deep. The greens, relatively level and easy to read, hold the ball well.

One can attack the flag often, and on many occasions this course permits golfers to take constant risks while driving powerfully for the green. But it is precisely these characteristics, which apparently make it an easy course, that constitute its principal risk. Do not let yourself be misled: play this seemingly innocuously open and level course carefully. The course penalizes the player with lakes, bunkers and outs, all strategically planned to interfere with the player's progress, especially when he feels it is safe to play overconfidently. If your attack is poorly planned or executed, you will immediately be penalized. If you care to earn a respectable score, never let down your guard. Play carefully and strategically.

The fifth, a par-5 of 587 yards, is a double dogleg to the left. A soft rough precedes the out to the left. The first shot requires a powerful stroke and should be aimed at the right side of the fairway. The second shot must also be powerful but always keep to the left side. At the landing area of both these shots, the fairway tightens, with two cross-bunkers on either side that quickly penalize any mistake in their direction. The shot to the green must be precise as well: in addition to the outs – one to the left and another at the back end – there are two bunkers that guard the left edge, and one lake to the right.

The three tees are traditional; each and every mark is perfectly centered. The tees, like the fairways, are planted in Kikuyo grass; the majority of the tees are wide and level. The roughs are planted in Bay grass, whose soft yet thick growth inhibits the golfer's swing. The trees there do not constitute a major hazard. The 78 bunkers are level and filled with gray river sand.

The greens, planted with bent grass, average 800 square meters in size. Although they are level, their large size and the cut of the grass, which often runs counter to the putt's path to the hole, mean that there is a strong danger of an unnecessary increase in your score. The most important lake on this course lies at holes ten and eleven and is the venue for a number of aquatic sports. There are other lakes of varying sizes along the course that, in one way or another, will influence the strategy and outcome of your game.

This golf course is characterized by a series of deceptive challenges: the first time you play there, you should do so carefully, because the risks are never obvious. These insidious hazards, brilliantly built into the design of the course, are meant to undermine your calm and confidence, so it is best to be aware of their capricious nature.

HOLE	PAR	HAND Women	HAND Men	⬛	⬜	🟥	HOLE	PAR	HAND Women	HAND Men	⬛	⬜	🟥
1	4	5	11	355	313	281	10	4	4	16	393	338	305
2	5	7	7	544	500	455	11	5	2	2	546	531	480
3	4	13	5	422	382	343	12	3	8	10	186	149	130
4	3	11	15	231	209	190	13	4	10	4	383	357	330
5	5	1	1	587	545	487	14	5	12	12	545	498	462
6	4	17	9	430	390	335	15	4	6	8	449	420	368
7	4	15	13	404	348	314	16	4	14	6	451	407	369
8	3	9	17	151	151	151	17	3	18	14	187	164	140
9	4	3	3	377	348	329	18	4	16	18	381	354	300
IN	36			3501	3186	2885	OUT	36			3521	3218	2884
							TOTAL	72			7022	6404	5769

		⬛	⬜	🟥
RATING		72.6	69.9	72.2

CORPORACIÓN CLUB CAMPESTRE DE MEDELLÍN
Medellín course

Address: Avenue 16 South # 34-950
Altitude: 1486 meters above sea level
Average temperature: 24 °C
Yards: 2764
Holes: 9, par-35
Designer: Karl Parrish (1924)
Medellín population: 2 026 000

This is one of the oldest courses in the country. When it was first built, the neighborhood lay on the outskirts of the city. With the passing of time, the city expanded and grew around it, but the course still conserves its beautiful landscape and natural features.

The course runs up and down a number of hills. The golfer must make use of all of his skill and control of the ball in order to play every kind of shot: with the ball above or below the level of his feet in a variety of uphill or downhill lies.

The most beautiful but the most difficult is the second, a par 5 of 551 yards, with a dogleg at the right and a lot of trees. The opening shot must be very straight in order to pass through the trees that border the stream that crosses the fairway. With a continuous out to the left, you have to deal with a cross-bunker on the right, at the 250 yards mark. The second shot must be aimed at the left of the fairway, because a number of trees close in the fairway on the right, giving rise to the dogleg. The green, located on the right, is placed amidst the trees and is very high: it is protected by two very deep bunkers on the right.

The drive-off tees are traditional: long and rectangular and sown with Bermuda 419 grass. The tees of the middle holes are lower, the fairways climb and the greens are elevated, in contrast with the rest, where the opposite is true.

The fairways, sown with Bermuda 419, are narrow and slippery: it is very difficult to control the bounces of the ball and you will always face a different stance at each shot.

The roughs, sown with a *trenza* grass that is not very thick, is made difficult by the great number of trees that frame the holes: laurel pines, eucalyptuses, palms, bamboos, mangos, oranges, *guayacanes* and *tulipanes*. Their overhanging branches and leaves become a great obstacle to your game: they knock the ball down and strongly punish any mistake.

The greens are difficult because they are elevated, smooth, small, hard and deceptive. Sown with Bermuda grass, they measure 250 square meters on average and are protected by 25 deep bunkers of gray river sand which, when it becomes wet, turns hard and heavy.

This course is a veritable oasis in the midst of a big city. In the leafy branches of its varied trees you will find a lively and noisy crowd of bluebirds, parrots, canaries, macaws, *mayos* and *siriríes*. As he walks along it, the player will come across spider monkeys, squirrels and iguanas, which happily scamper across the terrain. Perhaps its most surprising and exotic feature is a beautiful crystal-clear stream whose basin houses a variety of wild flowers, like *besitos, novios, azucenas* and *platanillos*.

HOLE	PAR	HAND	■	□	■	HOLE	PAR	HAND	■	□	■
1	3	7	121	112	105	10	3	18	121	112	105
2	5	1	441	422	388	11	5	2	441	422	388
3	3	15	151	134	117	12	3	16	151	134	117
4	5	5	412	404	329	13	5	6	412	404	329
5	4	11	360	349	317	14	4	12	360	349	317
6	4	7	375	367	281	15	4	8	374	367	281
7	5	3	563	555	494	16	5	4	563	555	494
8	3	9	185	170	139	17	3	10	185	170	139
9	3	13	156	148	126	18	3	14	156	148	126
IN	**35**		**2764**	**2661**	**2269**	**OUT**	**35**		**2764**	**2661**	**2296**
						TOTAL	**70**		**5528**	**5322**	**4592**

RATING		67.3	66.3	66.8

CLUB CAMPESTRE EL RODEO
Sede Macarena

Address: 41st street # 33-595, Rionegro
Altitude: 2120 meters above sea level
Average temperature: 17 °C
Yards: 6792
Holes: 18, par-72
Designer: Mark Mahannah; constructor Jaime Sáenz (1973)
Medellín population: 2 026 000

The course's classic design presents the golfer with an excellent challenge. As no other does, the course plays with the psychology of the golfer. It will make you feel various and contradictory emotions. If you can keep your head about you, you will be able to conquer the course.

The second, a par-3 of 196 yards, is sinister. In front of the tee you'll find a deep and difficult hollow; if the ball falls in this spot, you may need any number of shots to get free of it. The green is to the left side, with an out to the right. The stroke has to reach 170 yards in order to get free of the just mentioned deep and difficult hollow. Next, you will have to confront an immense and tricky green, guarded by four bunkers on the sides and beyond, not to mention the severely inclined rough. In other words, unless you land on the green, you will spend many shots getting out of whatever traps you fall into and you'll certainly miss your par.

The rectangular tees, planted in kikuyo grass, are higher than the fairways. Almost all of them are wide, measuring between 30 and 50 yards. Some holes are obviously uneven. The grass is a mixture of kikuyo, *trenza*, and Bermuda 419. The roughs are planted in the same mixture as the fairways. The surrounding, thickly-planted trees add to the course's difficulty, with many trees standing 30 meters in height! When nearby or underneath such trees it is usually impossible to set and focus your swing without a problem. Eucalyptus predominates, accompanied by pines, avocados, *guayacanes*, acacias, *arrayanes*, and native species like *sietecueros*, *uritos*, *curazaos* and *san joaquines*.

The course includes 88 bunkers, 27 of which are cross- bunkers, as well as nine medium-sized lakes situated in hollows near the fairways of fifteen holes, offering special penalties for those shots that fly off mark. There is also the "Cimarrona," a brook which meanders through holes four, five, twelve, fourteen, fifteen, and sixteen.

The wind blows against holes one, ten, eleven, and twelve and toward holes thirteen, seventeen and eighteen.

The exceptional weather and fantastic setting are propitious for a great variety of birds – Canadian geese, owls, hawks, canaries, cardinals and eagles, *pisingos*, *caravanas*, *tijeretas*, and animals like rabbits, squirrels, weasels, opossums, and bobcats. They are part of the richness of ecosystems that surround this course and contribute to its beauty.

The Macarena is a course of which we can assert, without question, that there will be moments of your game when you will be lifted into a realm that can only be described as sublime.

HOLE	PAR	HAND	🟦	⬜	🔶	🟥	HOLE	PAR	HAND	🟦	⬜	🔶	🟥
1	4	11	361	332	318	280	10	4	10	377	365	348	331
2	3	17	196	185	151	145	11	3	14	195	184	167	147
3	4	13	345	333	323	312	12	5	4	545	523	500	486
4	5	1	581	551	476	457	13	3	16	223	213	201	159
5	4	9	407	385	335	329	14	4	8	428	372	293	278
6	3	15	234	218	200	165	15	5	6	487	451	389	382
7	4	7	441	417	390	372	16	5	2	547	522	469	461
8	5	3	526	499	472	451	17	3	18	171	149	130	120
9	4	5	386	378	305	299	18	4	12	352	345	325	315
IN	36		3467	3298	2970	2810	OUT	36		3325	3124	2822	2679
							TOTAL	72		6792	6422	5792	5489
							RATING			73.2	71.7	73.7	72.1

ATLANTIC ZONE

Abutting the Caribbean, this zone constitutes a unique natural reserve abundantly rich in aquatic life. In this zone exist thirty-three natural parks and six flora and fauna sanctuaries. The zone counts on three golf courses – the Country and Caujaral of Barranquilla as well as the Campestre in Cartagena.

Lying along the west bank of the Magdalena River, within walking distance of the place where it debouches into the sea, Barranquilla boasts of being the northernmost river and ocean port in South America. The road system from there connects the coast to the interior of the country. Barranquilla has an international airport, which handles the transport of heavy cargo, and is also known as one of the country's most productive industrial cities. In the city itself you will find splendid examples of late 19th and early 20th century "Republican" homes, especially in the famous neighborhood of El Prado, where traditional architecture is combined with tall, striking modern buildings.

Barranquilla is the home of one of Colombia's most renowned carnivals, whose origins reach back to traditional Iberian celebrations that were later influenced by the traditions of the slaves brought from Africa. This all-out festival that goes on for four days non-stop is the highlight of the city's life and its international trademark. Every years, thousands of tourists flock to the city to enjoy the music and dancing of the colorful processions of the Carnival.

Cartagena, a colonial walled city, is considered to be the most beautiful and historic port of the Caribbean. It offers tourists the chance to explore eleven kilometers of fortified walls, forts and military installations, among them, the San Felipe de Barajas bastion, the best-conserved example of 17th century Spanish-colonial military architecture in South America.

By night Cartagena has a seductive atmosphere. Try a romantic horse and buggy ride along the narrow streets of the old city, or a delicious dinner or bohemian walk through the café-bar sector of the city. If discos are what you like, you will find a plethora of them, offering a wide variety of Caribbean music: some of the best are found in the new part of the city, where Cartagena's modern hotels, casinos, shops, and restaurants are located.

Close to Cartagena, you will find a stunning archipelago, the Rosary Islands, just one of Colombia's forty-six natural national parks: this natural reserve was created to protect one of the most important areas of coral reefs in the Caribbean.

Whether you go there for business or vacations, you'll be certain to encounter the capricious winds that blow endless numbers of yellow butterflies into Cartagena and eventually deposit them on its golf courses too. These butterflies give the golfer a marvelous feeling, lending a fantastic touch to an inspiring setting.

Corporación Club Lagos del Caujaral

COUNTRY CLUB BARRANQUILLA

Address: Puerto Colombia Road , km 7
Altitude: At sea level
Average temperature: 27 °C
Yards: 6522
Holes: 18, par-72
Designer: Northrop (1983)
Barranquilla population: 1 305 000

Dreamy sunrises, incomparable surroundings, beautiful beaches, delightful breezes, and the multicolored ocean are the features you will find when you play this course. Two absolutely distinct seasons – "winter" (the rainy season) and "summer" (the dry one) – change the characteristics of the course and the way you need to play on it.

Between May and November this course is wet and therefore heavy, thus the ball will not run well. The roughs are high, and a lot of rain falls but without much wind. From December to April, the course dries out while the winds pick up noticeably. At this time of the year, the fairways pack down and the roughs become dry. At such moments the wind can reach a speed of eighty kilometers per hour, which will affect the way you play the game: the wind can carry the ball up to forty yards in whichever direction it blows. Because of this tendency of wind interference, you have to be careful which club you choose.

The ninth, a par-4 of 410 yards, has an elevated, level tee from where you can see a panorama of this nine, which winds round the clubhouse. In the middle of the fairway, at 350 yards, stands an enormous cactus that can obstruct your progress during the game. After that obstacle you will see a high green surrounded by five bunkers. Although you have made it that far, you will not have escaped the wind, which of course can take your ball off-course. Remember this as you plan how and where you want to drop the ball.

Only two lakes are situated on this course. In summertime, however, only one lake appears, at the fourteenth. The elevated tees are planted in Bermuda grass 419; the fairways are planted in the same grass and are completely level, measuring on average between thirty-five to forty yards wide; however, holes one, two, ten, eleven, and fifteen are not quite as level and match the surrounding topography. The wide roughs can measure up to 50 yards. During summer, they are dry, compact, and without much grass. It is not easy to manage the ball as it bounces radically during this time of year. During winter a mix of native Bermuda and *cruceta* grass grows up to replace what died during the summer. The bunkers are filled with a worn, gray mountain sand. When it rains, the sand compacts and becomes quite hard; at this time of year you are recommended to go for a clean shot. Generally, the greens are level, planted with Bermuda grass 419 and a bit heavy, with the exception of those on holes four, five, and seven, which are a bit uneven. They measure 600 square meters, more or less. Foxes and iguanas roam the surroundings, where you will see coconut palms, pines, *matarratones* and other trees.

You will relax into a straightforward game without hidden tricks or traps; however, it is best not to underestimate the course, as it is designed to penalize the careless or overconfident golfer.

HOLE	PAR	HAND	🟦	⬜	🟥	HOLE	PAR	HAND	🟦	⬜	🟥
1	4	13	395	335	325	10	4	2	395	390	350
2	4	3	360	350	335	11	5	8	525	505	420
3	3	17	180	152	140	12	4	14	380	360	305
4	5	9	482	443	383	13	3	18	165	130	110
5	4	7	365	335	300	14	4	12	405	380	290
6	4	11	345	320	310	15	4	10	365	355	300
7	5	5	528	473	393	16	4	6	440	410	270
8	3	15	175	155	135	17	3	16	182	160	145
9	4	1	410	395	300	18	5	4	535	500	472
IN	**36**		**3130**	**2938**	**3591**	**OUT**	**36**		**3392**	**3190**	**2662**
						TOTAL	**72**		**6522**	**6128**	**5253**

	🟦	⬜	🟥
RATING (NORMAL)	70.0	68.9	71.1
RATING (WIND)	71.8	70.6	71.9

CLUB CAMPESTRE CARTAGENA

Address: Turbaco Road, sector Puente Honda. km 1
Altitude: 5 meters above sea level
Average temperature: 30 ºC
Yards: 7001
Holes: 18, par-72
Designer: Rafael and Jaime Villegas (1994)
Cartagena population: 952 523

Prepare yourself for a golf course where your game must adapt itself to the time of the year when you play, as the course changes dramatically with the changes of season.

From December until April, the weather is generally very hot and the area surrounding the course is arid. Such dry surroundings contrast with the lush and well-maintained golf course. Playing at this time of the year is challenging: the ball runs a lot, the sun pounds down, and the roughs lose their grass and erode. From May until November it is not so hot, and the heat, when it comes, is alleviated by frequent rains, which make the course softer and keep the ball from running so much.

Challenges and beauty characterize the entire course. A *samán* tree measuring twenty-five meters in height awaits you in the middle of the fairway, at 200 yards from the tee of the fourth, whose par-4 is 428 yards-long. There is a dogleg to the right and the fairway slopes from left to right. The tee-off should be played to fly right over the *samán* tree if you care to drive long, or you can aim for the left in order to bounce and run the ball, using the lie of the fairway. In the right rough, there are three *samanes* that are about eighty yards wide and thirty meters high. The green is guarded by bunkers on the right and the left. Make a stupendous drive and deliver it with awesome precision! Don't let the trees interfere with your concentration, and certainly don't rush past these wondrous gifts of nature. Few sacred moments compare to the one that occurs on this course at sunset on the green of this hole, when an intensely red sun descends over and then behind the *samán* trees.

Rock walls line the rectangular tees, which sit a bit above the level of the course and are planted in Bermuda 419. A few of them do not qualify as rectangular, since they are somewhat asymmetrical, insofar as their shape is adapted to the existing topography. The fairways, also planted in the same Bermuda grass, are uneven, with a variable topography. The forty-eight bunkers, generally flat and oval, are filled with large mining sand; from there you'll have to try to get the ball out cleanly, in order to avoid hitting your club against this thick, pebble-like sand. The greens, measuring on average 500 square meters and planted in Bermuda 328 and tifton dwarf, are tricky. The direction of the grain changes with the season and the wind; nonetheless, they are level, slow, and somewhat difficult to land on, especially during the summer months.

The course has three lakes that cross five holes. Canaries, wood ducks, geese, *tangas* and *peyares* constantly fly overhead. Also in abundance are the iguanas and lizards that climb the oak, laurel, mango, almond and tamarind trees.

The course's signature is the *samán* tree. It is recommendable to play the course both in both winter and summer, in order to experience the way that nature affects its design, offering you two highly distinct golf courses and golf games.

HOLE	PAR	HAND	🟦	⬜	🟥	HOLE	PAR	HAND	🟦	⬜	🟥
1	4	13	402	381	359	10	5	6	545	537	447
2	4	11	381	361	342	11	4	8	408	372	354
3	3	15	203	187	126	12	3	18	175	172	138
4	4	3	428	408	401	13	4	10	379	369	268
5	4	9	383	365	354	14	3	16	211	178	158
6	5	1	554	532	510	15	4	14	375	361	311
7	4	5	438	417	405	16	5	2	556	509	499
8	3	17	175	159	032	17	4	12	392	365	336
9	5	7	598	521	431	18	4	4	398	388	351
IN	**36**		**3562**	**3331**	**3060**	**OUT**	**36**		**3439**	**3251**	**2862**
						TOTAL	**72**		**7001**	**6582**	**5922**

RATING (NORMAL)	73.5	71.5	73.5

CORPORACIÓN CLUB LAGOS DE CAUJARAL

Address: Puerto Colombia Road, km 9
Altitude: 4 meters above sea level
Average temperature: 27-32 ºC
Yards: 6585
Holes: 18, par-72
Designer: Joe Lee (1970)
Barranquilla population: 1 305 000

Here you will encounter strong, very strong, winds, lots of water, abundant fauna and flora, and beauty everywhere. Do take care with the wind. Sometimes it is so fierce that you have to change the club as many as three times, or deflect your aim at an angle of between thirty and forty-five degrees. Follow this recommendation without any qualms; the wind will do the rest. If you put your hands forward and the ball in a stance to the right, you will shoot lower, which is the best technique in this weather.

This short course is located within a residential area: many of the holes have outs on both sides. The terrain has two levels. One is low, level, and has a lot of water; the other one is high, uneven, and offers a great view over the Caribbean.

From May to October you will find rain and light wind, but you can control the ball. From November to April the course's difficulty increases: although there is not too much rain, the winds pick up and interfere with ball's flight.

The tee of hole ones is thirty meters above the fairway, which makes for a perfect start and prelude to a great game. From that tee you can see the entire course, which encourages you to demonstrate your ability to hit a strong and exact drive: you'll see the ball's flight over the widest fairway of this course. You will find some cross-bunkers; however, they are not a big deal, since this par-5, at 490 yards, keeps you secure and at ease, so you can golf your best.

The most famous hole on this course is the fourteenth, a par-3 of 155 yards; at this hole the green is higher than the tee and the run up to the green is sloping. The fairway is uneven, with an out to the right and the ocean at the end. This hole is famous because the wind can change radically. Without wind to consider, a long golfer can play with a 9-iron; against the wind you can shoot with a 4-iron to get at the green. The wind that often comes from the ocean is at your back on holes one, four, seven, fifteen, sixteen, seventeen and eighteen; it crosses the fairways at holes two, three and five. On the rest the wind comes dead on.

The tees are traditional designs. Planted in Bermuda, they are wide and level in the low part, and uneven in the high part, like the fairways. The course has forty-nine bunkers, some of them deep and some not. The roughs change with the climate: when it is dry the roughs are very hard, with little grass and it is difficult to control the rebound; in winter the grass thickens and is often wet and heavy. This course has two large lakes that are the home of iguanas, geese, caimans, ducks, macaws, quails and *yuyos*. The outstanding characteristic of this course is that it poses provocative challenges: it is impossible not to feel stimulated. Nature-lovers will encounter a paradise here. When you are in the company of friends with whom you like to play, this is the perfect golf destination. For the beginner or the inexperienced player, this golf course is ideal.

HOLE	PAR	HAND	🟦	⬜	🟨	🟥	HOLE	PAR	HAND	🟦	⬜	🟨	🟥
1	5	11	490	480	445	405	10	4	2	430	425	380	375
2	4	1	410	400	300	290	11	3	16	210	170	165	110
3	4	9	375	375	360	350	12	5	4	520	495	480	435
4	4	7	370	330	300	300	13	4	6	360	325	265	240
5	3	17	140	125	110	110	14	3	18	155	140	120	115
6	5	3	555	530	455	450	15	4	10	360	345	330	285
7	4	13	370	360	330	320	16	4	14	335	325	310	285
8	3	15	175	155	150	130	17	4	8	430	390	375	370
9	4	5	395	375	345	335	18	5	12	505	475	405	405
IN	36		3280	3130	2765	2690	OUT	36		3305	3090	2865	2620
							TOTAL	72		6585	6220	5630	5310

	🟦	⬜	🟨	🟥
RATING (NORMAL)	71.1	68.9	67.5	69.6
RATING (WIND)	74.2	72.3	69.4	72.0

SAVANNA OF BOGOTÁ ZONE

"The Savanna," the term used throughout Colombia to indicate the countryside around its capital, Bogotá, is surprisingly not tropical. This zone is flat and tranquil, with a lot of sunshine; however, during the rainy season it is reminiscent of foggy London at certain times of the day, depending on the weather. In general the climate is warm to hot during the day but coolish to cold at night. The air is rarely humid. The savanna has a rare, even haunting, beauty, for the way that the vegetation meanders through the wooded areas. It is surrounded by majestic mountain peaks both on the east and west, which are divided by a complex series of inter-Andean valleys.

On the savanna many golf courses are surrounded by tall stands of trees, rocky hills, streams, and hot springs. Native plants adorn the courses, while thick, high trees look down from above and sometimes create unexpected challenges for the golfer.

The fourth largest city in South America, Bogotá is the political, economic, and cultural center of the country, as well as a modern and potent industrial one whose output continues to increase and improve. In Bogotá one can find both national and international financial institutions, as well as multinational companies and one of the most stable stock markets in Latin America.

Among her attractions one finds many museums which house collections of pre-Colombian, colonial, and modern art. The Candelaria neighborhood is of particular interest, with its well-conserved colonial architecture. Throughout the city you will find modern, well-stocked public libraries and sophisticated concert halls where it is possible to hear operas, zarzuelas and jazz recitals. Bogotá also hosts commercial and international exhibitions dedicated to books, arts and crafts, agricultural products and textiles, among others; during the bullfighting season bullfighters from Spain, France and Latin America perform in Bogotá. The rich offering of theater in Bogotá comes to a peak during the city's International Drama Festival, which is held every two years and features important theater groups from all over the world, which launch new works and revive old favorites. Bogotá offers world-class shopping malls, up-to-date movie theaters, excellent restaurants and sophisticated bars.

The savanna is home to twenty-four of the fifty golf courses in Colombia, fourteen of which are actually located within city limits, while the rest are located in the very nearby environs. All are easy to reach on well-maintained roads. The variety of vegetation and design of these 24 courses is impressive.

To play golf on the savanna of Bogotá is a lifetime's challenge, as both the altitude and wind conditions conspire against your talent and your stamina.

Bogotá Golf Club

CLUB DE GOLF LA CIMA

Address: Bogotá-La Calera Road, km 13,5
Altitude: 3000 meters above sea level
Average temperature: 10-15 °C
Yards: 6089
Holes: 18, par-70
Designer: Boris Sokoloff (1995)
Bogotá population: 6 700 000

This course is one of the world's highest and the single highest one in Colombia. To play here requires you to be in excellent health – there is considerably less oxygen at a high attitude, like that of Bogotá, than in the places where most courses are found. You must dress warmly and keep yourself hydrated.

The vegetation is typical of the high Andean region, that is, it is scattered and sparse in some places, but abundant in others. It is a punishing course, in part because of its natural obstacles. Looking northwards from the course you can see the valley of Sopó and the town of Zipaquirá. The second, a par-4 of 419 yards, is a typical example of what this course has to offer. The tee sits a bit higher than the fairway and has an out all along its border. To the left and in front there is a hollow containing an impenetrable wood of native trees that extends for seventy to eighty yards; to overcome this obstacle, it is wise to secure a high, straight and long first shot. For the second shot it is good to know that the fairway climbs and slopes to the left. The green is small, flat and a bit raised: the out is to the left and the bunker is to the right.

The seventeenth, a par-5 of 480 yards, cannot be attacked; the out to the left runs along its entire length. The first shot has to be a little to the right and the second shot should be landed well, in order to secure the green for the third shot: if the second shot is landed well, the green itself will lay a bit off to the left. On the last fifty yards before the green an overgrown briar patch lines both sides and narrows as it reaches the green, forming a gauntlet, fifteen yards- wide, through which the ball must pass in order to enter the green.

The classic tees, a bit higher than the level of the fairways, are planted both in kikuyo and a native grass that is well suited to the high altitude. The fairways are uneven, following the terrain along which they stretch. This is a very wet zone and the morning dew ensures abundant grass. For this reason the course has little need to employ any type of watering system.

The roughs do not have many trees, but are planted with a mixture of native grasses, which are long, and thin-leafed, and may grow very high at times. The roughs are bare and quite easy to gauge where the grass is sparse and short; however they do present difficulties at times, depending upon the lie of the golfer's ball. There are eight small lakes on this course that affect six holes. Additionally, there are twenty-five bunkers, many of which are designed to protect their greens. The sand is heavy and compacts easily. The greens are level, measure between 400 and 500 square meters and are spongy, so that they hold the ball well. This golf course, which is public, will require you to prove your mastery of the ball and ability to make strokes from a variety of difficult positions.

HOLE	PAR	HAND	🟦	⬜	🟥	HOLE	PAR	HAND	🟦	⬜	🟥
1	4	3	489	479	468	10	4	18	279	269	259
2	4	1	419	407	399	11	3	12	184	177	171
3	3	15	210	187	178	12	4	2	425	414	403
4	4	11	352	334	316	13	4	10	354	339	323
5	4	13	339	329	310	14	4	8	384	369	358
6	3	17	156	134	128	15	3	16	136	120	106
7	5	7	478	471	454	16	4	14	314	300	295
8	4	5	429	407	389	17	4	5	480	470	460
9	4	9	351	340	331	18	4	6	310	300	290
IN	35		3223	3088	2973	OUT	35		2866	2758	2665
						TOTAL	70		6089	5846	6638

RATING	69.7	68.7	74.5

CARMEL CLUB CAMPESTRE

Address: Diagonal 154 # 43-02, Bogotá
Altitude: 2600 meters above sea level
Average temperature: 18-20 °C
Yards: 6379
Holes: 18, par-70
Designer: Mark Mahannah (1971)
Bogotá population: 6 700 000

The course was designed to conserve and play up the natural features of the setting. Native trees and vegetation were part of the original vision: the ancient trees that were already there were preserved, in order to demarcate certain holes of the course. The course, in general, is short and level.

You'll begin the course with two par-3 holes. On the rest of the course there will be only three more of the same par. These holes are actually the most challenging on the course, and when you make par at these holes, you can finish the rest of the course well, maybe even below par.

The seventh, a par-4 of 407 yards, is straight, with out to the right along the entire length. From the landing area it narrows in the direction of the lake on the left and the bunker in front. The second shot needs to be thought out strategically, according to the location of the flag. The green has a steep slope to the left and is strongly guarded. You will have to place the ball below the flag, otherwise it will most likely take at least three putts to sink the ball.

The eighteenth, a par-4 of 396 yards, is decisive and will require that you make critical decisions. For instance, the tee-off should be centered between the two bunkers along each side of the fairway. On this shot you are granted very little margin for error: the shot to the green is dangerous – so don't tremble, be determined – in order to avoid the lake in front and quite close to the green, as well as the bunker that is to the left side. Even on the green the risks do not disappear: when you are putting, it is possible for the ball to end up in the lake.

The tees are rectangular platforms with all the marks on the same axis. Like the fairways, the tees are planted in kikuyo; they are level and very narrow. On average they measure twenty-five to thirty-five yards. Don't worry about the roughs as much as the surrounding trees that present a need for caution: acacias, *alcaparros*, candelabra pine and *romerones*, all tall and leafy, so much so that at some holes their branches obstruct the fairway and intercept the ball.

Of the seventy bunkers on this course those around the greens are deep; the cross-bunkers are fairly level yet large and the sand is yellow, loose and soft. The elevated greens, planted in penn cross, are very fast and hold the ball well, once you have got past the danger of the deep bunkers that guard them.

To play this course well, you will have to sacrifice distance for position. This course requires skill in the short game: the best strategy here is to play defensively and take good advantage of any opportunities that open up.

HOLE	PAR	HAND	🟦	⬜	🟥	HOLE	PAR	HAND	🟦	⬜	🟥
1	3	17	193	180	161	10	4	6	419	389	370
2	3	13	221	201	166	11	4	14	335	327	287
3	4	7	381	360	325	12	3	16	190	182	132
4	4	9	351	345	316	13	4	8	404	375	309
5	5	3	502	495	482	14	5	2	490	482	459
6	5	1	568	559	501	15	3	18	183	171	124
7	4	5	407	384	355	16	4	10	389	363	318
8	4	11	365	356	323	17	4	12	379	365	359
9	3	15	211	182	168	18	4	4	396	379	302
IN	35		3199	3062	2797	OUT	35		3180	3033	2660
						TOTAL	70		6379	6095	5457
	RATING								71.1	70.1	71.5

PUEBLO VIEJO COUNTRY CLUB

Address: Suba-Cota highway, km 7
Altitude: 2600 meters above sea level
Average temperature: 18 °C
Yards: 7410
Holes: 18, par-72
Designer: Boris Sokoloff assisted by Gary Player Design Company (1998)
Bogotá population: 6 700 000

Set in the vivid green cradle of the savanna – on a site where there once existed a cemetery of the local indigenous people – the course's design integrates both the presence and the layout of the Bogotá River: in various places and holes the river becomes part of the course. It is a modern, attractive and challenging course.

To the right of the Majuy mountain there is a depression called "tyhuaira," a word that in the extinct language of the Muisca Indians meant "song of the wind." On this course, the wind itself is an important aspect of the game. In January, February, and August, due to the "tyhuaira," northwest winds enter the course and are a force to be reckoned with, especially at hole number two.

The thirteenth, a par-5 of 597 yards with a dogleg on the left, is the most difficult and the longest. The Bogotá River borders its left side and one of its inlets forms the dogleg. The tee-off over the river needs to be oriented to the right of the fairway in order to avoid the water and land the ball strategically for the next shot. Much precision is needed in order to situate the ball in the center in order to avoid the river to the left and the lake on the right, at the entrance to the green! Sometimes it is preferable to sacrifice distance and choose a lower club in order to maintain a wider margin of error. The shot to the green needs to be careful, as a bend of the river runs around the back, while a lake and bunker to the right further narrow the entrance path. The green is long and narrow, with eucalyptus trees placed strategically to complicate the game.

The fourth, a par-4 of 393 yards, is straight. To the left of the tee lies a lake that follows its length until you are within 150 yards of the green. This lake and a cross-bunker on the right narrow the fairway, requiring a precise tee-off. Bunkers heavily guard the green. This is one of the largest courses in Colombia: 7410 yards. The watering system is computerized. The tees are traditional, rectangular, and large. The wide fairways, planted in kikuyo, give a lot, and the undulation is natural. The trees are used simply to demarcate; the course is not a forested one. The bunkers give the sensation that the grass is short. The sand, light and loose, allows for explosive shots. The greens are level yet difficult to read and are planted in bent grass, while the run ups to the greens are planted in kikuyo. The rough interferes, intentionally, with the fore-green, forming a neck that later opens and hugs the green, adding another difficulty to the hole.

They say that in times of wind the peaks of the mountains turn into music boxes with tunes that arrive as a whistling echo on the course and accompany the golfer as he plays his shots: we know that while music is the poetry of the soul, the golf on this course is all body and mind.

HOLE	PAR	HAND					HOLE	PAR	HAND				
1	5	10	514	514	488	456	10	4	13	415	405	395	365
2	3	18	186	171	155	138	11	3	15	224	213	182	140
3	4	4	470	470	435	386	12	4	9	430	390	346	311
4	4	16	393	378	362	323	13	5	1	597	586	550	518
5	4	14	392	392	354	320	14	4	7	436	413	390	370
6	4	8	397	374	344	307	15	3	17	185	185	169	151
7	5	6	572	572	545	515	16	4	5	470	470	433	390
8	3	12	252	220	187	157	17	4	11	447	434	404	366
9	4	2	480	441	411	390	18	5	3	550	540	472	437
IN	36		3656	3532	3281	2992	OUT	36		3754	3636	3341	3048
							TOTAL	72		7410	7168	6622	6040

RATING		73.2	72.2	69.4	72.0

CLUB EL RINCÓN DE CAJICÁ

Address: Central Highway to the North, km 26
Altitude: 2600 meters above sea level
Average temperature: 18-20 °C
Yards: 7150
Holes: 18, par-72
Designer: Robert Trent Jones, father. Alberto Serra, construction (1957)
Bogotá population: 6 700 000

"A wide terrain bordered on the east by the Bogotá river, a topography characterized by small hills, shallow valleys and a forest of tall eucalyptus and pines trees, with a certain number of hollows that can be easily adapted into lakes," was what Robert Trent Jones said of this course. In 1979 the *U.S. Golf Magazine* classified this extraordinary golf course as one of the world's fifty best. In 1980, the 28th edition of the World Cup was played here. The par-3 holes measure on average 210 yards, the par-4 holes 440 yards, and the par-5 holes 570 yards, on average. These characteristics alone would be demanding on any course at sea level, and here on Bogota's savanna the difficulty is compounded by the altitude and weather.

The sixth, a par-5 of 534 yards, has a dogleg to the left, an out along the whole length of the hole on the same side and three bunkers, equally on the left, located right in the landing area. With a long and high shot, you can play over the out, the trees, and the bunkers that are on the left side, opening up the possibility of reaching the green in two shots. Another way to play this hole is with a short stroke to the right side of the bunkers. The second shot is downhill and you can play it by shooting a high shot towards the green or a conservative shot to the center of the fairway, landing before the canal that crosses this hole in this part, which, like the lake, the two bunkers on the right and another on the left, serve to protect the green.

The seventh, a par-3 of 162 yards, has an out in the left: it is the most beautiful and at the same time one of the most difficult to play. A frontal lake stretches from the tee to the run up to the green. Halfway along the lake, on the left side, there is a colorful garden surrounded by a stone wall. The green is big and uneven with a downhill drop to the lake and three bunkers that protect the green on all sides. The rearmost one is the most complicated because it requires a downhill shot with the lake just in front. The tees follow a single axis; on average the fairways are forty-five yards wide. The tees, fairways and roughs are planted in kikuyu. On this course you can find extraordinary trees that are more than 100 years-old and stand between forty and fifty meters high, with very thick trunks and leafy branches. The eight interconnected lakes present frontal and lateral hazards on eleven holes. The Bogotá River meanders alongside the twelfth; in addition, a drainage canal borders the practice course and the seventh. The forty-four bunkers around the greens and the twenty-eight cross-bunkers are filled with fine river sand, gray, loose, and grass very light. The greens are fast; they measure on average 750 square meters and are planted in *poa* grass: they are uneven but receive the ball well.

To play in this exceptional climate with the great views and excellent playing conditions is an unforgettable experience and an unusual privilege.

HOLE	PAR	HAND	■	□	■	HOLE	PAR	HAND	■	□	■
1	4	8	415	392	358	10	4	1	453	430	401
2	4	14	423	394	356	11	5	3	537	499	442
3	4	10	538	497	464	12	4	13	404	378	464
4	4	4	380	359	337	13	3	15	201	180	159
5	3	18	211	180	145	14	4	11	393	379	353
6	5	2	534	512	470	15	4	9	419	496	372
7	3	16	162	136	110	16	5	7	601	563	538
8	4	12	388	361	334	17	3	17	200	186	172
9	4	6	446	415	382	18	4	5	445	407	376
IN	36		3497	3246	2952	OUT	36		3653	3418	3154
						TOTAL	72		7150	6664	6111

RATING		74.3	71.5	77.9

CLUB CAMPESTRE LOS ARRAYANES

Address: La Inmaculada Road, Highway to the North, km 14
Altitude: 2600 meters above sea level
Average temperature: 18-20 °C
Yards: 7002
Holes: 18, par-72
Designer: Fernando Gamboa (1978)
Bogotá population: 6 700 000

The level course has wide fairways, large lakes and an abundance of enormous, leafy trees. The greens are wide too, uneven, and very fast.

The most difficult hole is the seventh, a par-4 of 429 yards. Be careful with the club you choose for the first shot, since the landing area is very hard and the ball is liable to bounce radically. Make sure that your shot is precise and well-placed, to avoid falling in the cross-bunker on the left or the lake on the right, which crosses this hole at 260 yards.

The second shot is demanding too. To the right awaits a bunker, about thirty yards before the green. A bit farther along, on the same side and at the end, is a lake. The green is uneven and quite fast.

The eighteenth, a par-4 of 373 yards with a dogleg to the right, is an interesting hole. In front of the tee-off, to the right, there is a frontal lake that runs along the side of the hole; it is complemented by two cross-bunkers on the left and another on the right. For the second shot you will be facing the lake, quite close to the green and with two bunkers at the back, on either side.

The tees are rectangular, traditional in design and planted in kikuyo grass like the fairways. The latter are level, though at some holes they undulate slightly, and measure between twenty-five to forty-five yards wide.

Due to the deep shade cast by the great number of trees, the grass of the roughs is practically non-existent. Among those numerous trees you will encounter *arrayán*, acacia, eucalyptus, Roman pine, Candelabra pine, rubber, savannah rubber, *guayacán*, cherry, *alcaparro*, *aliso* and oak. *Copetones*, blackbirds, and other birds nest in these trees.

Geese, domesticated and wild ducks, and *tinguas* live around the six lakes on the course, all of which influence the playing of thirteen holes, presenting the golfer with frontal hazards in some places and lateral ones in others.

The greens are fast, uneven, hold the ball well and the dips are clearly visible; be careful on the greens because it is not easy to calculate the putt. The greens measure, on average, 600 square meters and are planted in bent grass. Surrounding the greens you'll find thirty-six bunkers, which are not very deep but are carefully situated to penalize careless shots.

In general, the course's twenty-eight cross-bunkers require long hitters to be very precise with their drives from the tee. This is a restful course which may be constantly attacked and will allow you to earn very good scores.

HOLE	PAR	HAND	🟦	⬜	🟥	HOLE	PAR	HAND	🟦	⬜	🟥
1	4	11	368	355	328	10	5	6	539	513	466
2	4	13	371	354	344	11	3	18	190	169	148
3	5	5	538	511	496	12	4	8	416	394	369
4	4	9	350	333	323	13	5	2	591	550	508
5	3	17	185	160	145	14	4	4	438	419	352
6	4	7	415	392	344	15	4	14	407	396	366
7	4	1	429	410	391	16	4	12	399	382	362
8	3	15	216	199	179	17	3	16	214	188	159
9	5	3	563	534	494	18	4	10	373	361	325
IN	**36**		**3435**	**3248**	**3044**	**OUT**	**36**		**3567**	**3372**	**3055**
						TOTAL	**72**		**7002**	**6620**	**6099**
						RATING			**72.7**	**71.2**	**73.6**

LOS LAGARTOS
David Gutiérrez course

Address: Diagonal 103 # 61-80, Bogotá
Altitude: 2600 meters above sea level
Average temperature: 18-20 °C
Yards: 7127
Holes: 18, par-71
Designer: Sr. Kuntz (1949)
Bogotá population: 6 700 000

Long hitters and professional golfers can score below par with relative facility on this golf course. You must use your driver confidently and shoot for the flag. This course allows you to play an aggressive game but exacts a stiff penalty for mistakes. The areas around the greens are difficult, uneven, and filled with bunkers. The greens hold the ball well, are honest and also have a lot of movement. The course has a classic design in a terrain which offers different types of holes. The nine holes on the mountain are undulating; while the other nine, on the lower part, are flat.

The most beautiful and at the same time the most demanding hole is the tenth, a par-3 of 207 yards. The level of the tee is below the fairway and a large frontal lake extends to the 103 yards marker; there the fairway begins to climb up to the green, where three large bunkers protect it. Certain obstacles complicate the shot here: the strong slope of the run up to the green, the green itself and the lake at its back. Make sure your ball lands below the flag, to avoid problems with the putt.

The sixteenth, a par-4 of 475 yards, has a dogleg to the left, an out along the entire length of the same side and a rough on the right. Tall trees border the whole of the fairway, so a good tee-off which places the ball on the right side of the fairway is required to guarantee a chance of reaching the green with the second shot, since the tall trees on the left close off the approach and leave you with no other alternative than the sacrifice of the next shot. The green is long, high, tight, making for a shot whose difficulty is heightened by two deep bunkers that guard it on either side. The markers on the tees, which are traditionally designed, follow the same alignment, although some are higher than others. The ample fairways are on average thirty-five to forty-five yards wide.

The tees, fairways and roughs are planted in kikuyo. During the rainy season the roughs are soft and thick, entangling the club so that it becomes difficult to control the ball. Even worse, any misplaced shot will most likely place the ball amidst the many large, ancient savanna-variety trees, with thick trunks and lots of leaves. Of the sixty bunkers, almost all of which are deep and filled with a light, loose rock sand, twenty-five are shallower and flatter cross-bunkers. The narrow greens measure on average 600 square meters: they are not level but easy to land on. Five of them are elevated, and the rest offer a clear view from the fairway to the green. Nine lakes, most of them large, play a role in the layout of ten holes.

Set in the midst of the city, this course allows you to appreciate Nature in all her ripeness, strength and glory. At the same time, it offers an optimum level of golfing thrills and challenges. The course is perfect for practice and training: it presents varied possibilities for playing your game, in ways that will test your strength and give you a great deal of satisfaction.

HOLE	PAR	HAND	■	□	■	HOLE	PAR	HAND	■	□	■
1	4	12	390	376	303	10	3	17	207	191	155
2	3	18	193	163	148	11	5	3	532	518	502
3	5	2	576	550	530	12	3	15	220	203	162
4	4	8	395	386	280	13	5	5	575	542	502
5	3	14	235	200	179	14	4	9	404	370	314
6	4	10	407	389	320	15	4	7	470	410	370
7	5	4	539	509	484	16	4	1	475	440	377
8	3	16	212	196	164	17	4	11	416	390	331
9	4	6	430	390	350	18	4	13	481	423	381
IN	35		3377	3159	2761	OUT	36		3750	3487	3074
						TOTAL	71		7127	6642	5835
						RATING			72.1	70.2	72.2

LOS LAGARTOS
Corea course

Address: Diagonal 103 # 61-80
Altitude: 2600 meters above sea level
Avereage temperature: 18-20 °C
Yards: 6135
Holes: 18, par-71
Designer: Fernando Gamboa (1972)
Bogotá population: 6 700 000

This is a golf course where short hitters can play very well; it gives them the chance to fight and even beat the long hitters. Ordinarily, most golf courses favor long hitters, whereas on this course the opposite is true. Here, distance and strength are not nearly as important as skill, finesse and precision.

This course is relatively narrow, short and level and the classic design takes advantage of the natural characteristics of the terrain. The key to the tee off is to place the ball in a strategic spot, generally by sacrificing distance. Although the shots to the green are straightforward, they require precision, since the greens are small, and the terrain around them is uneven and complicated. Two lakes will be encountered during the round: a medium-sized one which affects play on four holes, and a large one, where aquatic sports are practiced, which is part of the layout of the thirteenth to sixteenth holes, which are located around the perimeters of the lake.

The sixth, a par-5 of 504 yards, has a sharp dogleg to the left. The first shot must land at a distance of at least 230 but not more than 270 yards on a very narrow fairway. This shot must be very straight. A short shot will leave you facing the obstacle of the trees to the left; and a too long shot will send the ball into the right rough. The second shot must be played to land the ball before the lake that borders the right side and crosses the hole just before the green. The green itself is small, fast, well surrounded by trees and has both a lake and a bunker on the right side.

The fifteenth, 293 yards long, is a short par-4 with an incredible view of the green that is surrounded at the end by an immense lake. The traditional tees, designed in rectangular platforms with marks of a single alignment, are planted in kikuyo, as are the very narrow, level fairways that are eighteen to twenty-five yards in width, on average. The roughs have characteristics similar to those of the David Gutiérrez course.

This course has forty-seven bunkers, almost all of which are large: thirteen are cross-bunkers, level and superficial in depth. The sand of the bunkers is the same as that found on the David Gutiérrez course.

The greens are level, fast, and hold the ball. At some of the holes the weight of the surrounding trees makes the ground uneven, creating drops that are difficult to play. The greens measure on average 380 square meters. On this mature course the short and precise players will find a perfect opportunity to win. You need to play the ball with many effects to overcome any adversity. Each shot must be calculated with great strategy, as you do when playing chess. The shots must be clearly defined, and by no means allow your shot to run past the green; it will be difficult to recuperate from that error.

HOLE	PAR	HAND	🟦	🟥	HOLE	PAR	HAND	🟦	🟥
1	5	6	495	480	10	4	9	372	349
2	4	2	440	362	11	3	13	165	148
3	4	8	388	367	12	5	5	501	460
4	4	12	362	334	13	5	3	495	450
5	3	16	170	164	14	4	7	375	340
6	5	4	504	455	15	4	11	293	280
7	4	14	321	302	16	3	15	173	141
8	3	18	140	110	17	4	1	428	365
9	4	10	355	326	18	3	17	158	145
IN	36		3175	2900	OUT	35		2960	3678
					TOTAL	71		6135	5578

	RATING	🟦 69.4	🟥 72.0

CLUB CAMPESTRE HATO GRANDE

Address: Central Highway to the North, km 27
Altitude: 2600 meters above sea level
Average temperature: 18-20 °C
Yards: 7003
Holes: 18, par-72
Designer: Gary Player Design Co. and Boris Sokoloff (1995), construction, Fernando Gamboa
Bogotá population: 6 700 000

This golf course is open, level, and has wide fairways, without many hazards. The average player can enjoy this course. Some holes are adapted to the characteristics of the varied terrain: from long, straight ones to uneven short ones that punish any lack of precision. The constantly changing wind will be a big influence on your game.

The course's signature hole is the fourth, a par-4 of 337 yards, with a dogleg on the left and an out along the whole of the right-hand side. A lake with a stone retaining wall runs along the entire length of the left side. The fairway slopes a bit from left to right. This hole gives you the chance to choose your level of risk. You can decide to shoot directly over the lake to the green, which stands at a straight-line distance of 320 yards from the tee. In order to do this successfully, you need to hit the ball 280 yards: if not, it will fail to clear the lake. Another choice is to play to the right side of the lake. If you choose to play to the left, you will need to hit a longer shot, but it is also a more dangerous one. If you play to the far right your shot should be short in order to avoid the two cross-bunkers, as well as the heavily inclined roughs that are followed by the out. This second shot must be precise in order to cross the lake that enters on the left side and laps half of the green, the out on the right and the back, and the bunkers on each side and behind.

The sixteenth, a par-5 of 528 yards known as the "aircraft carrier", has an out on the right side, a rough to the left and a relatively high, level tee, with a little hollow in the fairway and a small area of tableland that should be the target of your drive. You must confront the lake and then the bunkers that protect the green.

The tees are rectangular and several holes have different marks for different categories of player. Some are high terraces buttressed by stone walls. The wide fairways are planted in kikuyo, some with subtle variations in the cut that distinguish them from the grass of the rough. The high, heavy, uneven rough is difficult to play because it makes it difficult to achieve the explosive, controlled shot that is needed to clear the vegetation. The few trees that grow on the course are relatively small.

All the holes are marked by water hazards. The lakes, with their gardens and papyrus plants, form an integral part of the landscape. The greens are planted in penn cross and measure 480 square meters on average. They are level, fast, and tricky; the deep bunkers, with their light, white, loose sand, guard them well. The cross-bunkers are very well placed to penalize any shortcomings of your shots.

It is not a punishing course but a rather friendly, tranquil, and enjoyable one, where you can practice your game in peace and pass the time in a beautiful environment.

HOLE	PAR	HAND					HOLE	PAR	HAND				
1	4	8	420	370	345	279	10	4	9	441	389	364	307
2	3	14	217	214	188	166	11	3	17	181	169	156	149
3	4	6	393	360	339	330	12	4	11	379	345	322	315
4	4	18	337	298	260	218	13	5	3	526	488	459	430
5	5	4	557	506	456	413	14	4	7	420	385	348	316
6	3	16	210	176	123	117	15	3	15	194	169	162	132
7	5	2	488	470	448	422	16	5	1	528	523	468	411
8	4	12	442	418	400	368	17	4	30	462	437	406	367
9	4	10	387	360	333	304	18	4	5	421	377	343	335
IN	36		3451	3172	2892	2617	OUT	36		3552	3282	2762	2762
							TOTAL	72		7003	6454	5379	5379
							RATING			73.4	71.9	74.9	71.9

CLUB POPULAR DE GOLF LA FLORIDA

Address: Parque La Florida, South side
Altitude: 2600 meters above sea level
Average temperature: 14 ºC
Yards: 3321
Holes: 9, par-36
Designer: Fernando Gamboa (1969)
Bogotá population: 6 700 000

This is a level and short golf course, with a lot of trees. Tall, ancient trees mark the course of each hole and present difficulties for the golfer. You must be careful to place the ball well and precise with shots to the green.

The layout of this public course respects the topographical features of the terrain. It has eight small lakes: one per hole at the fifth and sixth, and two per hole from the seventh to ninth.

The best hole here is number one, a par-4 of 386 yards, with a dogleg to the right. The first shot has to be straight and to the center because there are two cross-bunkers to the left and on the landing area trees in front and the right. You will probably have to sacrifice a shot by aiming for the run up to the green, because further on, between 75 and 45 yards to the green, are two bunkers, a small one to the left and a bigger one in the middle, and an out to the left; the terrain slopes to the left too. The green is narrow at the entrance and has a bunker on either side. You will need a lot of talent and precision to loft the ball onto the green.

Hole 5, a par-3 of 162 yards, has the tee a bit elevated above the fairway and is very narrow because the trees narrow the line of play. Between 123 and 148 yards you will find a little lake to the left. Take care with this shot, the branches on that side may deflect the ball into the water. The green is protected by bunkers flanking the entrance, and another deep one behind.

This course has a watering system and the drainage system is natural. The eastern part is surrounded by a marsh and the northern side has a lake that is used for recreation.

The tees, sown in kikuyo, are rectangular and square. The fairways are narrow and on average 40 yards wide; almost all are level, with undulations caused by the trees.

The roughs, cut at nearly the same level as the fairways, have a lot of acacia, eucalyptus and pine trees, set close to one another. Those trees are the major hazard of the rough. They often leave you no room to swing or block the path of the ball. Whatever it takes, you have to get out of there! Even if it generally means sacrificing strokes and distance.

The 33 bunkers of this course are made up of a white, loose, light pool sand but it tends to tighten when wet, making the shot more difficult.

The greens are sown with Bermuda grass, and measure 400 square meters on average. They are level, easy to land on and allow the ball to run true.

This course requires talent. You have to plan your strategy and follow it with care. Be ready for a great day of golf!

HOLE	PAR	HAND	■	□	■	HOLE	PAR	HAND	■	□	■
1	5	6	386	367	353	10	4	9	386	367	353
2	4	2	364	341	327	11	3	13	364	341	327
3	4	8	233	215	195	12	5	5	233	215	195
4	4	12	411	399	385	13	5	3	411	399	385
5	3	16	162	149	137	14	4	7	162	149	137
6	5	4	375	355	335	15	4	11	375	355	335
7	4	14	500	460	394	16	3	15	500	460	394
8	3	18	398	386	374	17	4	1	398	386	374
9	4	10	492	476	389	18	3	17	492	476	389
IN	36		3321	3148	2889	OUT	35		3321	3148	2889
						TOTAL	71		6642	6296	5778

RATING		72.1	69.4	73.6

CLUB CAMPESTRE LA SABANA

Address: Tibitó-Zipaquirá Road, km 6
Altitude: 2600 meters above sea level
Average temperature: 18-20 °C
Yards: 6345
Holes: 18, par-71
Designer: Mark Mahannah (1981)
Bogotá population: 6 700 000

This is a short narrow course on a rugged terrain. The design follows the natural topography of the land along the Bogotá River. The course is varied and slightly rolling, with valleys, rises and a number of dips adorned with the natural vegetation of the savanna. From the tee of number 2 one can see the dog-leg hole below and to the right, framed by the Bogotá River, a lake full of fish and five bunkers. Willow trees stand along the riverbank and the richly colored landscape blends into the misty mountains and their ancient salt mines. The water meadows of the Bogotá River provide another setting for the course at the points where holes 2, 3 and 4 wind their way through the low terrain amidst stands of acacia, willow and eucalyptus. The fish in the lakes and river attract ducks, herons and *tinguas*, among a great variety of native and migratory birds. If you are lucky you may catch sight of the majestic migratory eagles that fly over the lake at hole number 2 and swoop down to catch fish.

Hole number 5, set amidst a pine and eucalyptus forest that is enlivened by birdsong, requires steadiness and concentration. Your strategy should take into account the more than 30 meters-high trees that line the fairway and take care not to land in a wood from which it will be difficult to get out.

Hole number 7 is blind; it has a lake, bunkers, cross-bunkers and a forest, and requires you to shoot towards the mountains in the background. For the next shot, number 2, you must loft the ball onto the high green that is protected by four bunkers and a lake at the back – features that make the approach difficult but offer a compensating beauty.

Hole number 8, a par-3, climbs up to a green whose deceptively gentle slope and protective devices may cause unpleasant surprises unless you are cautious and concentrated.

From the level of the elevated tee at hole number 12 you can see the green so clearly that you are encouraged to attack the flag. Keep in mind, however, the wind, the woods to the left, the bunkers and the lake.

The tees are rectangular and planted in kikuyo, like the fairways, which are flat and undulating and have an average width of 35 yards. The greens are planted with bent grass and penn cross; they are rolling and slick. The Bogotá River and eleven lakes affect play on 13 holes of this course.

You must play this course conservatively and take great care with the placement of the ball: it is ideal for short hitters. If you are a passionate lover of nature, you will encounter a sublime mixture of light, shadow and color on this course, which further maintains a high standard of maintenance, design and personal service.

HOLE	PAR	HAND	🟦	⬜	🟥	HOLE	PAR	HAND	🟦	⬜	🟥
1	5	13	517	502	490	10	5	16	549	537	525
2	4	17	367	353	320	11	4	6	364	347	331
3	4	7	381	361	355	12	3	4	174	155	136
4	4	3	349	316	308	13	4	14	364	347	337
5	4	11	357	342	328	14	3	8	173	162	148
6	3	5	229	209	188	15	5	18	531	485	467
7	4	1	451	412	391	16	4	12	359	329	287
8	3	9	154	141	128	17	3	10	167	132	118
9	5	15	495	486	476	18	4	2	364	343	305
IN	36		3300	3122	2984	OUT	36		3045	2837	2654
						TOTAL	72		6345	5959	5638

RATING		72.3	70.7	74.7

CLUB CAMPESTRE EL RANCHO

Address: Highway to the North, 195th Street # 45-10
Altitude: 2600 meters above sea level
Average temperature: 18-20 °C
Yards: 6379
Holes: 18, par-72
Designer: Fernando Gamboa with changes by Jaime and Rafael Villegas
Bogotá population: 6 700 000

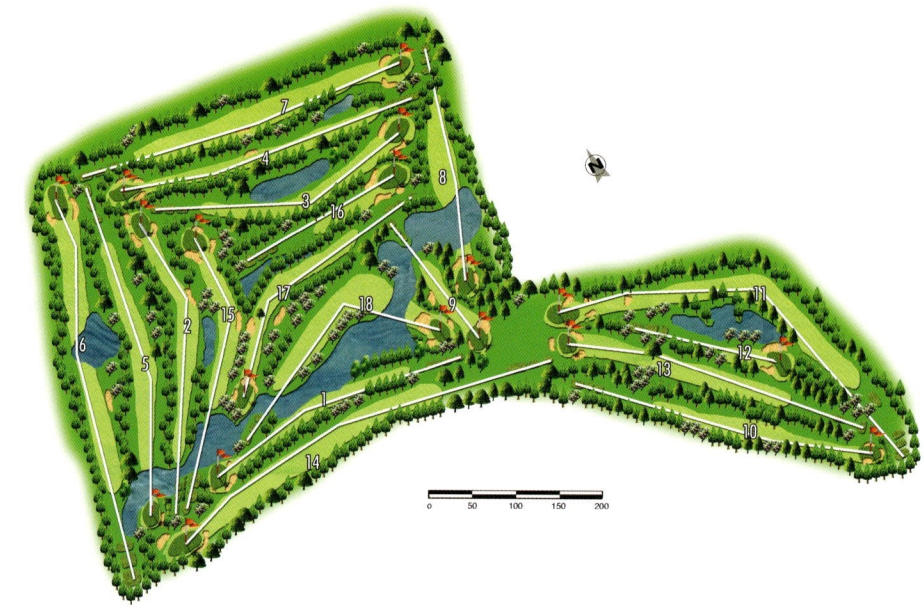

This is a short course with tight and slightly uneven fairways. As well as being strategically placed to challenge the golfer and form part of the technical and sporting design, most of the obstacles – lakes, bunkers, and trees – serve to protect him from the hazards that such a narrow course presents.

Hole number 5, a par-4 of 434 yards, requires you to tee off with the utmost precision. The tee is set between two lines of trees that give a certain feeling of narrowness but they widen a little on the fairway. Large trees fill the rough on the left for the whole length of the hole. The landing area is narrowed by an *arrayán* tree that crosses the line of play on the left side, while a lake enters from the right at a distance of 220 yards and is followed by a bunker. In short, the tee-off has to be very straight and aimed at the middle of the fairway. The second shot demands precision too, in order to avoid the lake that crosses in front of you and the large, long bunker that sits on the left side of the green.

Hole number 11, a par-5 of 526 yards, is a dog-leg to the left with an out all along the right side and a lake on the left, just where the hole bends. At its apex there is a stand of tall pines waiting to neutralize any attack that you attempt from this side. You must aim the first shot at the center of the fairway, taking care not to hit the ball so hard that it will run into the out at the back or so short that it will stop in front of the trees to the left. If you are a long hitter you can land on the green with the second shot, if you hit it hard and straight. If you prefer to play more conservatively, try to ensure that your second shot lands short of the bunker that is placed right in the center of the fairway, 75 yard before the green. In the shot to the green you must avoid falling into the two bunkers on the left, the two on the right and the out at the back.

All the tees are long, rectangular and elevated and many are flanked by hedges of pine. The fairways are between 25 to 30 yards wide. The roughs and tees are planted in kikuyo; the trees are a constant hazard, because if your ball enters the rough, you will probably have to sacrifice one or more shots. Deep bunkers protect the green; the cross-bunkers are shallower. Almost all of the greens, which are sown with bent grass and *poa*, are a bit elevated: they measure 422 square meters, on average. Ten of the greens are level while the rest are not. This course has many lakes: one, which is enormous, affects play on eight holes, while six smaller ones serve as guardians.

This course requires a strategic game. You must weigh each shot carefully, in order to avoid problems with the following one. Concentration and a thorough knowledge of the course are the keys to a good round here.

HOLE	PAR	HAND	🟦	⬜	🟥	HOLE	PAR	HAND	🟦	⬜	🟥
1	4	13	366	349	332	10	4	8	392	386	366
2	4	11	370	355	338	11	5	14	526	508	436
3	4	7	345	326	309	12	3	12	190	175	162
4	4	5	403	394	373	13	4	6	395	374	336
5	4	1	434	415	361	14	5	2	574	557	436
6	5	9	486	467	449	15	4	18	352	333	314
7	4	3	424	406	388	16	3	10	217	202	190
8	4	17	295	280	267	17	4	16	352	335	322
9	3	15	184	171	156	18	4	4	351	336	322
IN	36		3307	3163	2973	OUT	36		3349	3206	2884
						TOTAL	72		6656	6369	5857
						RATING			73.7	72.8	73.8

CLUB SAN JACINTO

Address: Highway to the North, Chía Road, km 19, east side
Altitude: 2600 meters above sea level
Average temperature: 18-20 ºC
Yards: 3485
Holes: 9, par-36
Designer: Boris Sokoloff
Bogotá population: 6 700 000

This is a course on a flat terrain with a lot of movement, characterized by a modern landscape design of great beauty which incorporates many gardens, bodies of water and small cascades.

Built in the midst of a condominium, big lakes and bunkers are strategically placed to protect the homes. The layout is out and back, that is, the first four holes move away from the clubhouse, while the next five return to it in a parallel line. The tees are elevated above the fairway and each marker is set at a different height and offers a different distance and line of play. Hole number 3, a par-4 of 393 yards, gives a good idea of the spirit of this course. The tee is raised a bit above the fairway; the golfer has to plan the first shot carefully, aiming at the right side, even if it means sacrificing a bit of distance, in order to avoid the lake that runs along the whole of the left side from the 180 yards marker onwards. The ball should land near the first of the four bunkers placed on the right, at a distance of 150 to 80 yards before the green.

The second shot demands exactitude both in distance and direction. About seven yards before the green the fairway is crossed by a lake that nearly surrounds the green, only leaving a narrow spit of land at the back that connects it to the following hole.

The entrance to the green is narrow but it widens towards the back, where it slants from right to left. Be careful when the flag is placed on the left of the green, for the ball may easily land in the water!

On hole number 8, a par-3 of 195 yards, the tee is high, and the whole of the left side is flanked by the entrance road to the condominium, which is an out. It has an immense 100 yard-long bunker, with a total area of 1800 square meters, that covers most of the fairway, only leaving a little lane to the right. The green is long and narrow and has a rough at the end.

The fairways are uneven and demand concentration and finesse to hit and land the ball advantageously. The roughs and fairways are planted in kikuyo. The roughs are undulated, heavy and complex and the ball almost always up in a place that makes playing it difficult. One needs to be patient and controlled.

Trees do not line the holes. Instead, they are demarcated by bunkers, lakes and outs. The overall sensation is of playing golf in an immense and well tended garden

HOLE	PAR	HAND					HOLE	PAR	HAND				
1	4	11	407	361	322	286	10	4	12	407	361	322	286
2	3	15	191	175	140	103	11	3	16	191	175	140	103
3	4	9	393	393	353	310	12	4	10	393	393	353	310
4	5	1	617	578	543	505	13	5	2	617	578	543	505
5	3	13	193	178	142	127	14	3	14	193	178	142	127
6	4	7	429	383	330	290	15	4	8	429	383	330	290
7	5	5	541	514	481	449	16	5	6	541	514	481	449
8	3	17	195	195	164	129	17	3	18	195	195	164	129
9	5	3	519	457	405	361	18	5	4	519	457	405	361
IN	36		3485	3234	2880	2560	OUT	36		3485	3234	2880	2560
							TOTAL	72		6970	6468	5760	5120

CLUB CAMPESTRE GUAYMARAL
Course 1 - Lagos

Address: Central Highway to the North, km 18
Altitude: 2600 meters above sea level
Average temperature: 18-20 °C
Yards: 6924
Holes: 18, par-72
Designer: Boris Sokoloff and Gary Player Design Company (1992)
Bogotá population: 6 700 000

On Lagos (or Guaymaral 1) you will encounter a course of a classic design, with fairways surrounded by lines of tall, robust trees, frontal hazards, and a lot of water.

Taking masterly advantage of the natural topography of the terrain, with its innumerable springs of water and characteristic vegetation, the designer harmonized these elements to build a beautiful course, which is abundant in water and technically impeccable in accordance with his style.

The area in which this course is located is very humid. It is 30% rainier than its neighbor, course 2. It often happens that when it rains on course 1, you will not see even a single threatening cloud on course 2

On the first nine holes you will find seven frontal water hazards and many flowering trees.

Hole number six, one of the most renowned on this course, sets the tone for the rest. It borders the highway and has a green that is very special by virtue of its beauty, difficulty and the water that surrounds it.

The tee of hole number seven, a par-4 of 433 yards, stands in a privileged position above the fairway and permits a clear view to the tee. You must place the first shot on the right of the fairway and reach at lest 210 yards to avoid the lake that crosses the hole and runs along its left side. For the second shot you will have to watch out for another lake that barely leaves the narrowest stretch of fairway on which it will not be possible to land the ball. For this reason you have to execute a decisive stroke to the green. It is one of the most complicated on the course: you have to play very well to get a par.

To the left of hole number 12, a par-3, you will find a stand of eucalyptus trees and on the right a water hazard, beautiful to be sure but a definite complication.

The fairways and roughs are sown with kikuyo and the grass on the latter is cut higher to make them more difficult. Many native varieties of trees surround this course's holes.

The greens, planted in *poa annua*, are flat and straightforward, with an average size of 400-500 square meters. In accordance with the criterion of the designer, the hazards must appear along the route to the green, while the green itself should give you an opportunity of a good putt.

This course is a challenging one, but it also offers a balanced chance to find satisfaction.

This is the kind of course that attracts you to golf and then turns you into a fanatic.

HOLE	PAR	HAND	🟦	⬜	🟥	HOLE	PAR	HAND	🟦	⬜	🟥
1	5	13	522	491	439	10	4	16	388	353	342
2	4	17	388	377	326	11	4	6	376	354	308
3	4	7	422	412	354	12	3	4	197	183	170
4	4	3	419	406	344	13	5	14	533	519	474
5	3	11	180	171	125	14	4	8	446	435	421
6	4	5	385	374	338	15	4	18	364	355	313
7	4	1	433	418	364	16	3	12	160	153	147
8	3	9	182	171	161	17	5	10	527	516	459
9	5	15	548	540	480	18	4	2	454	443	384
IN	36		3479	3360	2931	OUT	36		3445	3311	3018
						TOTAL	72		6924	6671	5949

RATING		72.9	71.9	74.1

CLUB CAMPESTRE GUAYMARAL
Course 2 - Links

Address: Central Highway to the North, km 18
Altitude: 2600 meters above sea level
Average temperature: 18-20 °C
Yards: 7339
Holes: 18, par-72
Designer: Mark Mahannah
Bogotá population: 6 700 000

Nothing comes easily on a golf course, and on this one, even less. This is an open course with few trees, an uneven terrain and slick fairways and greens that require precise strokes. Pay attention to the way the ball bounces after it lands.

The different features of this course were carefully planned from the start in order to form part of an integral strategy for the planning and execution of the game. This modern concept is uncommon in Colombia and the course incorporates the rigorous guidelines laid down by the PGA Championship standards for design.

Hole number 2 is particularly long: 437 yards. It has a dogleg to the left that is formed by the pronounced angle at which the lake breaks into the fairway. For the first shot, choose either a long iron or a middle wood to place the ball in the right spot. Rose bushes line one whole side of it. Hole number 5, a par-4 of 426 yards, has four cross-bunkers to the left that narrow down the landing area for the tee shot. The second shot has a lake on the left. Protected by three bunkers, the long, tricky green has an extremely narrow entrance and is set to one side.

Hole number 15, a par-5 of 600 yards, has a dogleg to the left. There is a lake that enters the left side of the fairway at 225 yards from the tee and crosses it 95 yards from there. The golfer must hit a strong drive to the right of the fairway. To guarantee a comfortable second shot, the first shot needs to be very straight. Pay attention to the lake on the right and the two large cross-bunkers on the left. The green is small and not easy to land on: a counter slope makes it even more difficult. Surrounded by five bunkers, the hole has a diagonal entrance.

All the fairways narrow down to a width of 25 to 30 yards at the landing area, at around 260-70 yards. This demands a precise tee-off for both scratch and professional players, who will also have to face cross shots to narrow greens. Nonetheless, the course's design is also enjoyable to the average golfer.

The main defenses of the courses are the roughs, which are light and heavy, according to the cut of the grass. The 98 bunkers are deep and filled with washed cliff sand; there are also nine grass bunkers to prevent the ball from falling into the lakes. The lakes are lateral hazards for the short hitter, but for the long hitter who attacks the course they become frontal ones.

The greens measure between 700 and 900 square meters: they are specifically designed to repel anything short of a perfect shot, like those on the Pine Hurst course in the United States. They also have inner corridors that force the golfer to deal with up to four dips on a single putt. This course is tempting for the player who goes for the long stroke and requires a game that is professional, technical and precise. April is the most beautiful time of the year on both courses.

HOLE	PAR	HAND	🟦	⬜	🟥	HOLE	PAR	HAND	🟦	⬜	🟥
1	5	5	592	562	502	10	4	5	589	563	498
2	4	4	437	410	350	11	4	4	410	378	320
3	4	4	390	370	331	12	3	3	201	171	130
4	4	3	201	167	138	13	5	4	398	365	302
5	3	4	426	392	348	14	4	4	403	357	292
6	4	4	402	370	323	15	4	5	598	560	500
7	4	3	188	162	130	16	3	4	467	428	359
8	3	5	568	532	470	17	5	3	179	149	110
9	5	3	417	392	345	18	4	4	473	436	377
IN	**36**		**3621**	**3357**	**2937**	**OUT**	**36**		**3718**	**3407**	**2888**
						TOTAL	**72**		**7339**	**6764**	**5825**
						RATING			**74.6**	**71.4**	**71.3**

BOGOTÁ GOLF CLUB

Address: Tocancipá-Zipaquirá Road, km 2
Altitude: 2600 meters above sea level
Average temperature: 17 °C
Yards: 6824
Holes: 18, par-72
Designer: Fernando Gamboa (1987)
Bogotá population: 6 700 000

This golf course, narrow and short, requires a careful strategy, sound handling of the ball, good placement of tee shots and precise shots to the green.

The most difficult is number 2, a par-5 of 583 yards, which is bordered by an out along its whole length. Its narrow fairway is closed in on the left by a lake that runs from the 175 to the 320 yard marker and followed by two cross-bunkers, one on each side, that further tighten the fairway.

The second shot has similar characteristics: two cross-bunkers, one to the right and the other to the left, and a lake further on, are the obstacles that you must confront here. The approach to the green must be impeccable, since all flanks of it are protected, either by the a lake on the right side or the four bunkers that surround it. The green has two levels; if you are unlucky enough to miss the one where the flag stands, you may easily have to make more than three putts.

Hole number 16, a par-5 of 498 yards has a dogleg to the left, and an out along the entire left side. Immense trees surround this hole. Play your first shot to the right; keep in mind the bunker that flanks the landing area on that side. For the second shot the best strategy is to play to the right side of the fairway, short of the lake. In this way you will avoid facing the trees during your shot to the green. This shot to the green will require precision to avoid the bunkers on either side and the out at the back.

The tees, of traditional design are rectangular and planted in kikuyo, like the fairways. The latter are flat and narrow, and between 20-30 yards in width. The grass in the roughs is sparse and offers little resistance. Instead, you will find different types of trees: eucalyptus, acacia, pine, willow, highland rubber and *sietecuero*.

The greens are planted in a combination of Bermuda 328, bent grass, and *poa*: they are easy to read and measure on average 500 square meters. They are level, hold the ball well and are protected by very deep bunkers.

The cross-bunkers are not as deep and penalize any error in the sand shot.

This course is balanced: it never penalizes a good shot, but does not reward a poor one either. It is demanding in terms of precision and control of the flight of the ball. Some holes require the golfer to employ controlled fades or draws.

HOLE	PAR	HAND	🟦	⬜	🟥	HOLE	PAR	HAND	🟦	⬜	🟥
1	4	5	383	361	343	10	4	12	370	348	326
2	5	1	583	574	482	11	3	18	166	153	142
3	3	15	200	175	135	12	4	6	445	432	392
4	4	13	401	384	320	13	5	4	468	457	447
5	4	9	364	340	315	14	4	14	406	394	317
6	5	3	565	541	446	15	3	16	181	168	136
7	4	7	394	384	374	16	5	2	498	487	439
8	3	17	179	169	160	17	4	10	382	366	308
9	4	11	396	383	370	18	4	8	453	421	357
IN	**36**		**3465**	**3311**	**2945**	**OUT**	**36**		**3369**	**3226**	**2864**
						TOTAL	**72**		**6834**	**6537**	**5809**

	RATING			72.3	71.3	72.9

LA PRADERA DE POTOSÍ

Address: La Calera-Sopó Road, km 5
Altitude: 2650 meters above sea level
Average temperature: 18-20 °C
Yards: 7716
Holes: 18, par-72
Designer: Mark Mahannah (1999)
Bogotá population: 6 700 000

This course was built to the standards of quality of the USGA. Following a landscape design concept, the trees are located in strategic places but do not form avenues that limit the holes, as in a traditional design. The topography is varied and planned from the start. The dunes and sinks that you see are not only meant to condition the strategy of the game: they are also an integral part of the aesthetics of the design and further serve to optimize the drainage of the course. The tees are independent, with different routes from each marker and different shapes, according to the layout of the hole. On all holes the fairways narrow at the landing area. If you are a long player, prepare yourself for a precise tee shot and a skillful shot to the narrow and crossways greens. It is a course that has been designed to test the strategy, strength, precision and courage of the scratch player. It offers the possibility of a pleasant and enjoyable day of golf for the average player.

The irrigation system is computerized and satellite-controlled. The roughs, sown with kikuyo, are heavy and high and play a fundamental role in the design. They were made wide to protect the homes that form part of the residential development that lies around the course and also clearly mark the borders of the fairways and highlight their features.

The greens hold the ball well, are uneven and measure 650 square meters on average. Most of them are elevated. They are sown with bent grass-penn cross, which is suitable for the cold climate and resistant to frosts.

Hole 3, a par 3 of 211 yards, is a good example of what happens on the course. It has four tees, arranged at different levels and angles, which permit a clear view towards the green. The fairway is beautifully laid out: a lake borders the right side and there are big trees on the right. The green, set diagonally at the end, has a deep bunker.

Hole 4, par-4, 456 yards, the black markers of the tee are placed on an island in an ornamental lake. They are high and afford a very good view over the hole. The first shot must be strong and aimed at the middle of the fairway. To the left a lake borders almost the entire length of the hole; on the its banks there is a beach bunker that runs from the 220 to 270 yard marker. On the right side, at 275 yards, there are two cross-bunkers. The second shot must be long and straight. The lake on the left and the two bunkers penalize any shot that is weak or off course. The green, longer than it is wide, also has the decorative elements that characterize this course.

This course has 84 bunkers filled with a loose, light, soft sand that allows for an explosive shot. On this course you will enjoy a profound feeling of spaciousness and tranquility as you contemplate the many textures and colors of the beautiful landscape that surrounds it.

HOLE	PAR	HAND	■	■	□	■	HOLE	PAR	HAND	■	■	□	■
1	5	4	595	567	530	490	10	4	7	485	444	409	376
2	4	8	449	405	354	304	11	4	13	422	388	339	292
3	3	14	211	170	135	109	12	3	15	219	190	163	144
4	4	12	451	419	381	342	13	5	1	578	545	508	416
5	4	2	456	428	391	356	14	4	11	470	433	398	370
6	5	10	602	566	497	449	15	4	9	448	414	367	337
7	4	16	402	372	332	298	16	3	17	215	194	177	159
8	3	18	205	180	146	122	17	5	5	585	574	559	500
9	4	6	457	403	359	321	18	4	3	466	416	378	341
IN	36		3828	3510	3125	2791	OUT	36		3888	3598	3298	2935
							TOTAL	72		7716	7108	6423	5726

SAN ANDRÉS GOLF CLUB

Address: La Punta-Funza Road, km 2
Altitude: 2600 meters above sea level
Average temperature: 15-18 ℃
Yards: 7145
Holes: 18, par-72
Designer: Thompson and Jones; R. H. Russell, construction (1945)
Bogotá population: 6 700 000

The name of this course pays homage to Saint Andrews, the birthplace of golf. Crowded with great trees that frame each hole or obstruct the path of the ball, this is a relatively flat course that requires a great deal of precision in the tee shot, when you must always consider the conditions for the following one, since almost all of the holes are or tend to be doglegs.

Hole 6, a par 3 of 184 yards, is especially pretty. The elevated tee affords a good view of the whole of the green and what lies before it: a frontal lake, some 60 to 65 yards wide, which breaks into the fairway after the 95 yard marker and runs to the fore green. The green itself is a bit long, with bunkers that protect its flanks and a barrier of very tall trees behind which form part of the beautiful landscape of the savanna.

The eleventh, a par-4 of 429 yards, is likewise pretty but also demanding. A lake runs along its left side and the right side is bordered by a rough full of trees. The tee shot must be long and a little to the right, to avoid the lake, but without sending the ball into the rough or you will have to sacrifice a stroke. The approach to the green also requires strategy: keep clear of the lake and the bunkers on the right – one forty yards short of the green and the other bordering it. Play to the center but without attacking flag. The eighteenth, a par-5 of 557 yards, has a double dogleg, first to the right and then to the left. It is wide and requires a long tee shot aimed to the right of the fairway. Avoid the trees and cross-bunkers on the left, which complicate the second shot. If your first shot goes right, you can try to hit the green in two strokes with a long secure drive and may wind up with a birdie or even an eagle. If you are not so bold, place the ball a little to the left in order to guarantee a comfortable and straightforward shot to the green. The green is completely surrounded by seven bunkers of different sizes, which requires a very well executed approach.

This is a classic course, on which the characteristics of the game are determined by the topography. The tees are rectangular, a bit elevated and sown with kikuyo. The fairways, also planted in kikuyo, are not too narrow but the surrounding trees make them seem tighter than they are. The majority are level, with gentle undulations. Two lakes influence play on five holes. On holes 6, 7, and 13 they present frontal hazards and on holes 11 and 14, lateral ones. The 88 bunkers, 33 of which are cross-bunkers, are generally located in the landing area of the tee shot. They are filled with a fine, white sand which offers little resistance. Bunkers are located around the greens; they are deep, but the sand makes them relatively easy to get out of. The greens, 660 square meters on average, are fast. Most are level and hold the ball and allow for straightforward shots to the flag. They are planted in bent grass. In short, this course requires strategy and precision.

HOLE	PAR	HAND	🟨	🟦	⬜	🟥	HOLE	PAR	HAND	🟨	🟦	⬜	🟥
1	4	12	421	416	410	363	10	4	13	413	409	377	370
2	5	2	575	544	523	462	11	4	1	429	422	418	362
3	3	18	196	188	180	172	12	5	3	574	556	539	477
4	4	8	428	407	396	383	13	3	15	202	196	196	189
5	4	10	429	412	402	392	14	4	11	393	388	383	323
6	3	16	184	176	152	142	15	4	9	410	403	395	356
7	5	4	507	498	487	474	16	3	17	220	185	178	172
8	5	6	517	510	499	445	17	4	5	458	440	434	376
9	3	14	232	224	216	193	18	5	7	557	530	509	443
IN	36		3489	3375	3265	3026	OUT	36		3656	3529	3429	3068
							TOTAL	72		7145	6904	6694	6094

RATING	🟨	🟦	⬜	🟥
	72.3	71.5	70.4	72.9

CLUB MILITAR DE GOLF

Address: Highway to the North, km 30, Sopó
Altitude: 2600 meters above sea level
Average temperature: 18 °C
Yards: 6716
Holes: 18, par-72
Designer: Fernando Gamboa (1978)
Bogotá population: 6 700 000

If you are a cerebral player then this is the course for you. Here you will have to be willing to take risks when the circumstances are favorable. The tee shots and shots to the green require a great deal of precision

This course is generally flat but has undulations that may help you to place the ball in a good position or equally force you into an odyssey in the rough.

During the outward nine you'll need to play conservatively. This course rewards tee shots to the center of the fairway and penalizes slices. The inward nine has an out to the left along its whole length, but offers many temptations to the aggressive player.

The greens are expertly maintained: they are soft and easy to land on. They are protected by bunkers and lakes that influence play on eight holes.

Hole number 7, a par-5 of 508 yards, has a dogleg to the right; the tee-off is narrow with a long line of eucalyptuses on the right and an equally long line of pines to the left. On the latter side, one immensely tall and full-branched eucalyptus interferes with the recommended line of play when you try to avoid the cross-bunker located 220 yards from the tee. If you are a long hitter, a good tee shot will leave you with a chance to reach the green on the second shot; but you will face the risk of the lake and the deep bunker that severely penalizes any misreading of the distance or direction. If you are a short hitter, the second shot is decisive: a central cross-bunker, 100 yards from the green, will encourage you to aim for the left but a badly played shot may land you in the lake. The long green is flat and narrow at the entrance and wider but more undulating at the back: you need a very precise approach shot.

Hole, a par-3 of 192 yards, is one of the most beautiful. The tee is raised and will force you to choose your club carefully. With a frontal lake, an out to the left as well as at the end and willow trees to the right, this hole requires you to be very precise about length and direction. The green is large, slopes from back to front and has a beautiful garden at the back. It is also protected by three bunkers in front and one to the right. This tempting beauty will try the nerves and composure of any player.

This course requires concentration, skill and a flexible approach to game strategy: you may be aggressive or cautious. Whatever you do you are sure to enjoy the beautiful natural landscape of this part of the savanna.

HOLE	PAR	HAND	🟦	⬜	🟥	HOLE	PAR	HAND	🟦	⬜	🟥
1	1	4	442	424	406	10	4	2	421	409	398
2	4	9	346	323	304	11	3	6	192	169	164
3	5	5	535	524	462	12	4	12	345	334	293
4	3	13	178	162	142	13	4	10	367	356	312
5	4	17	423	405	393	14	5	4	519	503	486
6	3	17	175	144	125	15	4	14	324	306	292
7	5	15	508	487	473	16	4	8	381	364	348
8	4	11	404	391	374	17	3	18	182	164	148
9	4	3	441	426	337	18	5	16	503	492	481
IN	36		3452	3286	3052	OUT	36		3224	3086	2884
						TOTAL	72		6676	6372	936

RATING	71.6	70.0	73.2

COUNTRY CLUB BOGOTÁ
Los Fundadores course

Address: 129st street # 15-02
Altitude: 2600 meters above sea level
Average temperature: 15 °C
Yards: 7161
Holes: 18, par-72
Designer: John Van Kleek (1946)
Bogotá population : 6 700 000

The course is for the versatile player. It is carefully designed so that the player can use all types of club during one round. It will require all of his skill to manage the ball and precision and talent when putting.

Planted in bent grass, the best for the climate and altitude of Bogotá, it is classic in design, with level fairways and tree-filled roughs.

Hole number 9, a par-4 of 447 yards, requires the use of strategy. At the tee-off you will be facing an intimidating lake: the challenge is clear the lake but land short of a *second* one, which lies 260 yards from the tee. From the area between the lakes, you will need to make a precise shot to the green, of 170 yards at least, in order to cross the second lake and avoid the bunkers either side of the green. When shooting for the green use the flag to guide where you land your shot; otherwise you may need more than three putts to hole it.

Hole number 18, a par-5 of 551 yards, may turn around the results of a tournament. Begin this hole confidently, using a driver to hit for the center of the fairway. Without losing your nerve, pay attention to the four bunkers on the right and the out to the left. Afterwards, loft the ball onto the green, aiming for an eagle. This shot must cross the lake in front of it. Avoid the lateral bunkers and remember that your ball will land on a big, fast green where the slightest mistake may be costly.

The outstanding characteristics of this course are its long elevated, rectangular tees; level fairways, measuring between 25-35 yards wide; and wide, punishing tree-filled roughs.

The sixty-seven bunkers which surround the greens mostly have a protective function. They are large but not very deep. The cross-bunkers penalize a poorly executed shot. The greens are elevated, level, and very fast, measuring on average 650 square meters. They have large and visible dips and some even have two levels: a poor shot to the green can be expensive. Two large lakes influence the play on 11 holes and constitute the water hazards on this course. In the roughs are magnolias, eucalyptuses, rubber trees, pines, cedars and *fresnos*. The most difficult holes are the par-3's because of their length and the bunkers that guard the greens. In general, however the course is playable, provided that you take care to place the ball in the right spot, handle the medium irons well and are able to work such effects as fades and draws. But be careful not to land short on the sides or the back of the greens, because recovery will be complicated.

Even though this is a fair course that rewards or penalizes according to your level of execution, it is not easy to break par on it. Play it strategically and above all, with a lot of patience.

HOLE	PAR	HAND	🟦	⬜	🟥	HOLE	PAR	HAND	🟦	⬜	🟥
1	4	8	522	491	439	10	3	15	388	353	342
2	5	4	388	377	326	11	4	9	376	354	308
3	4	14	422	412	354	12	4	3	197	183	170
4	4	12	419	406	344	13	5	1	533	519	474
5	3	16	180	171	125	14	4	13	446	435	421
6	4	10	385	374	338	15	3	17	364	355	313
7	3	18	433	418	364	16	4	11	160	153	147
8	5	2	182	171	161	17	4	7	527	516	459
9	4	6	548	540	480	18	5	25	454	443	384
IN	36		3479	3360	2931	OUT	36		3445	3311	3018
						TOTAL	72		6924	6671	5949

	RATING	73.7	72.3	75.7

COUNTRY CLUB BOGOTÁ
Los Pacos y Los Fabios course

Address: 129st street # 15-02
Altitude: 2600 meters above sea level
Average temperature: 15 °C
Yards: 7161
Holes: 18, par-72
Designer: John Van Kleek (1946)
Bogotá population : 6 700 000

This course is specially designed for those who regard golf as merely a weekend hobby or for players with a handicap of more than 23.

In general terms, this is a short course without lakes, where the bunkers and small greens constitute the true difficulty.

Here the long hitters can enjoy hitting the green in one stroke on the par-4's and in two on the par- 5's. Nevertheless, it may become an ugly nightmare if your short game is off, because the greens are very small and high.

Paradoxically, the hole that presents the greatest challenge in terms of the scorecard is the shortest. Hole 17 is only 115 yards-long, but its four flanks are protected by the deepest and most difficult bunkers on the entire course.

On this course the tees are short and rectangular. Like the fairways, they are planted in kikuyo grass, while the greens have bent grass.

The 52 bunkers, all filled in yellow cliff-sand, are clearly visible but deep and very difficult. The difficulties that the bunkers present have more to do with the nature of the traps themselves than their location: once you fall in it is difficult to get out and for this reason they lend interest to the holes on the course.

The Country Club has two golf courses: the "Fundadores" and this one, both of which offer a wealth and variety of trees – immense magnolias, tall leafy *urapanes*, many types of eucalyptus and pine, rubber trees, *alisos*, *saucos*, willows, *cajetos*, *sangregados*, oaks, *cuyaros*, jasmines, cherries, *guayacanes*, cedars, walnuts, *fresnos*, and different types of holly.

Tempting to long hitters, the course is short but complicated, especially around the greens, because of their location and the deep bunkers that guard them. Holes such as number 2, 6 and 17 demand caution.

In this course any hole may become easy or difficult, depending on the tee shot. It is an ideal place to learn the game and perfect for practicing short and sand wedge shots.

HOLE	PAR	HAND	🟦	🟥	HOLE	PAR	HAND	🟦	🟥
1	4	6	351	334	10	4	9	379	358
2	3	16	159	148	11	3	15	157	139
3	4	10	337	319	12	5	1	511	485
4	3	18	154	140	13	4	7	383	363
5	4	14	284	270	14	4	5	403	391
6	4	4	392	374	15	4	11	360	341
7	5	2	501	482	16	4	13	357	339
8	4	8	350	339	17	3	17	115	108
9	4	12	308	295	18	5	3	469	449
IN	35		2836	2701	OUT	36		3134	2973
					TOTAL	71		5970	5674
					RATING			67.2	71.2

SERREZUELA COUNTRY CLUB

Address: La Mesa Road, km 1
Altitude: 2600 meters above sea level
Average temperature: 15-18 °C
Yards: 7325
Holes: 18, par-72
Designer: Jaime and Rafael Villegas, with the technical assistance of The Golden Bear Co. (1994)
Bogotá population: 6 700 000

The challenges here include the long distances, large unreadable greens, and many water and sand hazards.

The tee shots must be precise. For long hitters the landing areas have cross-bunkers that punish the slightest error. There are also lakes that do the same job. The roughs add another difficulty: they are undulating and have a heavy cushion of grass, so that the ball exits weakly and without much control.

The design of the course is adapted to the features of the terrain. It is very long and the fairways are level, with a width of 40 to 45 yards. The greens are immense, with an average area of between 900-1000 square meters. Crosswinds affect your game, especially on the eighteenth, where you also have to be careful at the approach to the green.

The par-3's are the most complicated because of their length. They have punishing lakes to the front or the side and the big greens are surrounded by bunkers.

At 258 yards, the sixteenth is the longest par-3 on the course. The lake surrounds the tee and stretches along its left side until you are 110 yards short of the green. This lake is followed by two cross-bunkers, between 100 to 90 yards short of the green, which penalize poor shots. If you are not a long hitter, it is better to play this hole as a short par-4: locate the ball a bit to the right with the tee shot. This will allow you a comfortable shot to the green and even the possibility of making par. Hole 11, a par-3 of 197 yards, is breathtaking in its beauty. A lake runs along the whole length of the left side to the back of the green and it also has a waterfall and elegant gardens that create a narrow path of fairway on the right. The green is long and narrow and is surrounded by three bunkers.

The traditional rectangular tees are planted, like the fairways, in kikuyo. The roughs are undulated and balls almost always land in a difficult position. Also sown with kikuyo, they are cut into a light and heavy rough. Ten lakes, which are fed by the Ramada canal and the Subachoque River, affect the playing of holes 7, 9, 11, and 12. The 99 bunkers are filled with a well sand from Tocancipá that is light and loose and has an even consistency. Of these, 45 surround the greens, affording them strong protection and requiring precision of the golfer. Nearly all of the 54 cross-bunkers are located at the landing area for the tee shot, to force precision, especially for the long hitter. The greens are planted in bent grass: they are large and fast and hold the ball but make it roll a lot. Nevertheless, their deceptively flat appearance makes them hard to read.

This is a course that allows you to show off your golfing talent but it is demanding as well. To play it well, you will need skill and strategy, without forgetting precision, of course.

HOLE	PAR	HAND	🟨	⬛	⬜	🟥	HOLE	PAR	HAND	🟨	⬛	⬜	🟥
1	4	9	406	391	366	332	10	4	12	401	397	382	368
2	4	15	363	359	340	309	11	3	8	197	192	171	163
3	3	11	217	217	217	140	12	5	2	612	569	529	479
4	5	1	618	559	532	506	13	4	14	396	368	334	313
5	4	7	485	425	394	345	14	4	16	338	332	318	236
6	4	3	460	445	421	309	15	5	4	575	545	505	459
7	5	13	541	507	468	424	16	3	10	258	226	200	179
8	3	17	197	163	147	140	17	4	18	381	366	339	308
9	4	5	468	456	436	394	18	4	6	412	404	384	354
IN	36		3755	3522	3321	2899	OUT	36		3570	3399	3162	2859
							TOTAL	72		7325	6921	6483	5758

RATING	🟨	⬛	⬜	🟥
	73.6	71.8	69.7	71.4

COFFEE ZONE

Located in the midst of the cordillera of the Andes, this region affords the chance to undertake a journey through a variety of exotic climes: high peaks of perpetual snows, volcanoes, mist forests, rivers and lakes, hidden valleys with fertile soils ideal for growing all sorts of crops. There are few places on the planet where you may encounter such a rich variety of ecosystems within such a relatively narrow compass.

The Quimbayas, the indigenous group who lived in this region in pre-Colombian times, were superb goldsmiths and ceramists and have left behind a rich cultural legacy. Their masterpieces were the fabulous gold "*poporos*" that may be seen today in Colombian museums, a gourd-shaped vessel used to hold the lime that was mixed with coca leaves in their ancient rituals. This region was settled, for the most part, by land-hungry emigrants from the Department of Antioquia – adventurers, romantics and bohemians of inexhaustible mental agility, ambition, courage and endurance. Entering as cattle drovers or treasure hunters, they brought their customs and traditions with them in the accordion-shaped leather shoulder-bags known as "*carrieles*", which they still use: a paradoxical mixture of devout Catholicism, strong family loyalty, a great sense of humor, entrepreneurial spirit, hard work… and (at times) even harder play at dice, cards and fighting cocks.

The vernacular architecture associated with the colonization of the coffee zone by settlers from Antioquia has awoken the interest of academics and artists, because of its creative and skillful use of local materials, adaptation to a difficult terrain and beautiful integration with the natural landscape. One of the Departments found in this region is known as the Quindío, a name which derives from the ancient indigenous word for the earthly paradise. And that is perhaps the best description of what the visitor will feel when he travels through the coffee zone. A recent and highly successful innovation which takes advantage of these features is the ecological tourism that allows visitors to stay in the beautiful hacienda houses of the coffee plantations of the region. Among the attractions of this region are the National Coffee Park, the Guadua Museum, the Quimbaya Museum (of anthropology), the Matecaña Zoo and outings to its hot springs and snow-covered mountain summits. There are also bullfights, the Manizales theater festival, the harvest festival in Pereira and the coffee festival in Armenia.

This magical oasis is the setting for the ritual of golf as it is played on the marvelous courses of Manizales, Armenia, and Pereira, the respective capitals of its three Departments. On these golf courses the inherent challenges and rewards are offered by Nature herself. Whatever the difficulties, each hole and each stroke offers a marvelous spectacle of color and fragrance that has few peers in the world of golf.

Club Campestre de Armenia

CLUB CAMPESTRE DE ARMENIA

Address: El Edén Road, km 10
Altitude: 1475 meters above sea level
Average temperature: 21 °C
Yards: 6588
Holes: 18, par-72
Designer: Álvaro Tula, first 9 holes (1965). Redesigned
Fernando Gamboa, second 9 holes (1991)
Armenia population: 305 550

This course is ideal for the player who wishes to develop his skill at different kinds of shots and master strokes made difficult by an uncomfortable terrain. It requires a game that emphasizes a careful placement of tee shots and precision in the approach to the green.

Number 18, a par-4 of 423 yards, is a nice hole with an out to the left. The tee shot must be aimed so as to fall between the guadua bamboos, whose branches invade the fairway from the 220 yard marker to the green, forming a narrow arch which is known here as "*La Arquería*" or "Archway". For this shot, as for a soccer goal, you have to be strong, precise, resolute and straight, in order to place the ball right in the middle of the fairway. At this point the fairway dips down and later rises to a high green, well protected by bunkers. In this shot several factors have to be taken into account.

First, that the terrain descends and the ball flies a bit to the right and flat. Second, that the pressure of the dip forces the stroke downwards, creating a short, low flight. Third, that if you go slightly off course, the ball will hit the guaduas and begin a long series of rebounds

Most of the tees, which sown with Bermuda 419, are of the traditional rectangular kind. The bunkers are deep and are generally positioned to penalize bad shots to the green or complicate the approach. The fairways are wide but short: There are four big lakes that cross 11 holes and occupy natural depressions: the verges are covered by tall native grasses.

To reach the greens you must consider the way the ball will bounce along them. Planted with bent grass, the greens are semi-hard, well tended and relatively flat. But be careful! They are hard to read, because of the subtle undulations that deceive the golfer.

The vegetation of this course displays the enormous richness of nature in this region. Ornamental trees like *guadua*, *samán*, acacia, *yarumo*, walnut, cypress, cedar and bottle palm are complemented by fruit trees – mango, guava, *grosella*, *guamo*, *pomarrosa* – which attract wild birds, squirrels, iguanas, foxes, and rabbits. Other fruit trees are planted in the roughs and produce quantities of oranges, mandarins and lemons.

The natural characteristics of this region are evident on this course, which is set in a privileged location of farms and coffee plantations. To play golf in such a place is a special experience: a peaceful and enjoyable adventure that is impossible to forget.

HOLE	PAR	HAND	🟦	⬜	🟥	HOLE	PAR	HAND	🟦	⬜	🟥
1	4	9	349	294	271	10	4	8	411	397	366
2	3	5	146	134	122	11	4	14	390	344	325
3	5	1	552	516	469	12	5	2	535	481	455
4	4	11	365	347	320	13	4	12	383	371	342
5	3	15	208	177	153	14	3	16	223	209	199
6	5	5	481	470	424	15	4	10	394	356	312
7	3	13	232	214	294	16	3	18	152	126	133
8	5	7	500	456	407	17	5	6	465	410	400
9	4	3	372	362	290	18	4	4	423	408	339
IN	**36**		**3212**	**2970**	**2650**	**OUT**	**36**		**3376**	**3001**	**2834**
						TOTAL	**72**		**6588**	**6071**	**5484**
						RATING			**72.1**	**69.4**	**73.6**

CLUB CAMPESTRE DE MANIZALES

Address: Vereda El Rosario. Manizales-Chinchiná Road
Altitude: 1450 meters above sea level
Average temperature: 22 °C
Yards: 6602
Holes: 18, par-72
Designer: Rafael and Jaime Villegas, first 9 holes.
Fernando Gamboa, next 9 holes
Manizales population: 372 000

This course, relatively level given its mountainous situation, requires precision and expert control of the ball.

Its sixty-two bunkers represent the greatest difficulty of the course. The sand is hard and compact, which makes it difficult to control the ball. You will have to draw on all of your talent to achieve a well executed shot.

The greens are planted in Bermuda and measure 400 square meters. You will need to putt skillfully, because, despite being level, they are hard, small and tricky and well protected by bunkers. Gauge the bounce of the ball with care. At times you must start the ball rolling on the run up to the green to achieve the approach you are striving for

One of the outstanding features of this course is the way its design respects the natural topography of he terrain. For the experienced player, its main attraction are the constant challenges posed by the short shots and by the need to place the tee shots in the correct position. For the rest, the course offers a tranquil game, an incomparable landscape and a mountainous setting that is magical who those who want to enjoy golf as well as play it.

The rectangular tees are elevated above the fairways. The latter are a bit uneven and undulated. Both tees and fairways are planted with Bermuda grass.

The grass found in the roughs is *trenza* and is cut to the same level as the fairways. The roughs are not difficult: when you fall into the rough, a recovery shot is easily accomplished.

One of the most difficult holes is the fourth, a par-4 of 380 yards that has four lakes. The first is in front of the driving tee and widens a little to the right. The second is on the left of the landing area for the tee shot. The third crosses the whole width of the fairway, from 70 to 10 yards before the green. The fourth is to the right of the green. These lakes require a lot of precision from the golfer: they allow no room for errors. Your drive must be long and precise. The second shot is on a downhill lie, which makes it hard to loft the ball. Both the lakes and the out at back oblige the golfer to be exact with the stroke.

This course has seven small lakes where ducks and fish live. The vegetation reflects the enormous natural wealth of the region. Among the many ornamental trees, you will find leafy *samanes*, *guaduas*, acacias, *ceibas*, *tulipanes*, and *guayacanes*. There is also a rich array of birds, lizards and small mammals, most of them native to the region.

This part of Colombia exudes an enviable spirit of determination and hard work, reflected in the orderly plantations of coffee, plantain and fruit trees that stretch to the horizon. The fertile mountainous setting, with its mosaic of greens and rich natural blessings, contribute to the enormous pleasure you feel when you play golf on this course.

HOLE	PAR	HAND	🟦	⬜	🟥	HOLE	PAR	HAND	🟦	⬜	🟥
1	5	3	570	533	440	10	4	8	377	337	320
2	3	17	160	140	130	11	3	16	180	150	140
3	4	1	416	406	296	12	4	2	411	390	303
4	4	5	380	334	330	13	4	10	353	316	300
5	3	15	181	177	154	14	5	6	540	530	438
6	5	11	467	460	410	15	4	12	349	339	325
7	4	13	376	316	310	16	5	18	530	498	430
8	4	7	382	370	320	17	3	18	177	147	132
9	4	9	391	380	315	18	4	14	362	343	330
IN	36		3323	3116	2705	OUT	36		3279	3050	2718
						TOTAL	72		6602	6166	5423

RATING	🟦	⬜	🟥
	71.4	70.0	71.3

CORPORACIÓN CLUB CAMPESTRE DE PEREIRA

Address: Pereira-Cartago Road, km 18
Altitude: 1415 meters above sea level
Average temperature: 23 °C
Yards: 6695
Holes: 18, par-72
Designer: Fernando Gamboa, first 9 holes (1979). Charles Mark Mahannah and Jaime Sáenz, second 9 holes and rearrangement of the course (1986)
Pereira population: 490 000

This course's design respects the naturally uneven topography, which creates blind shots because of the deep hollows and dips and are turned into hazards sown with native grass on some holes. In this variety of grass, tall and long-leafed, the ball stays hidden and the stroke becomes difficult.

Hole number 2, a par-4 of 393 yards, is a clear example of what this course has to offer: the tee is on the left side of the San Isidro lake. The fairway has a pronounced rise that reaches a small plateau and a sloping rough on the left. Your first shot must be long and high, and aimed to the right of the fairway, which allows you to pass the lake and crown the hill. There you will find a big cross-bunker in the middle of the fairway. The next shot, to the green, will be blind: the green sits below the plateau. There is a brook 50 yards before the green, while to the left you will find a native forest that borders the same side of the green. Here the shot must be precise and strongly hit. Be careful of the two bunkers on the right. On the green you will face a new challenge: two clearly visible levels that require great skill and concentration with the putter. This is a complicated hole, but don't get upset: not all of the holes offer so many challenges.

The tees are traditional and planted in Bermuda 419, as are the fairways, which roll naturally. The greens measure, on average, 550 square meters and are planted in tifton dwarf and Bermuda 328. They are semi-hard and in general the ball rolls well, but they are difficult to read because of the way they run and the direction of the grass.

The bunkers are filled with thick river sand which does not compact, so that it allows you to hit the ball explosively without sacrificing precision. There are some 50 in all: some level, some deep, and most guarding the greens. Four large lakes, which cross and make life difficult on 11 holes, adorn the course and also provide water for its irrigation system.

A concert of birdsong accompanies the golfer during the game as the birds fly about and roost in the branches of the *samanes*, acacias and *ceibas*. Wild animals, like rabbits, iguanas, squirrels and little foxes can be seen scurrying for cover in the thick vegetation as golfers pass by. The surrounding trees include *guaduas*, *tulipanes*, *guayacanes*, palms, breadfruit trees, *caracolíes*, *lluvias de oro* and *urapanes*. Indifferent to the passage of time, the turtles sunbathe, while the eagles fish the lake. The golfer will encounter a great variety of fruit trees: mangos, guavas, *guamos* and *pomarrosas*.

This course offers a challenging experience that mixes both the pleasure and the pain of the game; regardless of your score, you cannot fail to enjoy yourself in this unforgettably beautiful and tranquil setting.

HOLE	PAR	HAND	🟦	⬜	🟥	HOLE	PAR	HAND	🟦	⬜	🟥
1	5	3	606	591	561	10	4	14	351	325	308
2	4	5	393	371	342	11	3	18	187	159	137
3	3	17	162	151	133	12	5	10	487	464	441
4	4	13	424	396	371	13	4	4	419	397	348
5	4	9	381	371	323	14	4	8	398	386	346
6	5	1	561	544	424	15	3	16	198	182	165
7	4	7	346	346	310	16	4	6	429	407	361
8	3	15	154	139	115	17	4	12	370	343	326
9	4	11	416	398	332	18	4	2	413	397	361
IN	**36**		**3443**	**3307**	**2911**	**OUT**	**35**		**3252**	**3060**	**2793**
						TOTAL	**71**		**6695**	**6367**	**5704**

| | | | | | | **RATING** | | | **72.4** | **71.2** | **73.3** |

SANTANDERS ZONE

The Department of Santander is in the northeastern part of the country. On the west it is bounded by the Magdalena River, which is responsible for the numerous marshlands and warm wet valleys of the region. This Department also has rugged and extensive mountains, whose topography lend it an exceptional physical beauty. The biggest petroleum refinery in the country is found here, in the city of Barrancabermeja. Santander is a Department where you can go from arid tablelands to high Andean moors in a matter of hours.

This is a good area for adventure sports, especially in the canyons of the Fonce and Chicamocha Rivers, where rafters shoot the rapids

The golf courses of the Campestre and Ruitoque Clubs in Bucaramanga – the capital of this Department – take advantage of the richly diverse topography of the region

With their well preserved colonial architecture, the towns of this Department are a major tourist attraction. Don't miss Barichara, with its cobblestone streets, adobe houses, stone churches, and flowering gardens. Another example is Girón, famous in the past for its gold mines and tobacco industry. This town conserves a splendid architectural heritage.

Bucaramanga, the capital, known as the "the city of parks", stands out for its lively cultural and economic activity and is also the seat of important universities.

The Department of "Norte de Santander" which lies on the frontier with Venezuela, is beautiful and full of contrasts. High mountain ranges lie close to hot-climate prairies and the humid tropical region of the Catatumbo jungle.

Cúcuta is the capital. This city has the vigorous commercial enterprise of a major frontier city. It also has a strong cultural life that revolves around museums, libraries and educational institutions. There, the Club Campestre is an ideal place for business conferences.

Another city of historical interest is Ocaña, the site of the famous constitutional convention that led to the creation of the modern state of Colombia.

Initially a single region, the Santanders produce tobacco, quina bark, sugar cane, rice and African palm: mining and petroleum are also important. It is also known for its hand-rolled cigars and crafts products, especially rustic furniture and work in stone, fique fiber and ceramics.

Club Campestre de Bucaramanga

CORPORACIÓN RECREATIVA
TENNIS GOLF CLUB CÚCUTA

Address: Between the bridges Elías M. Soto and San Rafael, Cúcuta
Altitude: 320 meters above sea level
Average temperature: 33 °C
Yards: 2888
Holes: 9, par-35
Designer: Alberto Ronderos and Julio Polanía (1973)
Cúcuta population: 685 000

This is a short, demanding course. Because the ball runs easily, there is a high risk of outs on the fairways. The greens are not easy to land on on. At times stopping the roll is the work of Titans.

Hole number seven, a par-4 of 328 yards, an interesting one. The drive from the tee will need your maximum precision: the recommendation is to land on the left side of the fairway, some 65 to 120 yards short of the green, where you can find a stand of trees on the right. The shot to the green will require prudence. A good part of the line of play is blocked by an enormous tree whose branches are so big and thick that they may intercept the ball and drop it into the water of a small brook which runs to the right side of the fairway and crosses the run up to the green at about 55 yards from it. Keep in mind that at the end of the green you will find two bunkers and an out. Don't forget that on this course the ball bounces hard.

The tees are rectangular and planted in Japanese grass. On holes one and nine the women's and men's markers are in line. Holes 2, 3, 5, 6, and 8 have different tees for each category of player and on the fourth the markers are on different levels.

The fairways are level and planted in a combination of Japanese, Bermuda, and Angleton: the average width is between 30-50 yards.

The roughs are sown with the same combination of grasses as the fairways; there are many trees, such as mango, *chiminango*, *guanabana*, cherry, and oak. All of these trees are utilized by animals and birds for food or nests. Squirrels, iguanas, canaries, woodpeckers, parrots, hawks and white eagles may be seen around the course.

While playing this round the player will encounter eight frontal lakes that influence play on holes 3, 4, 5, and 9. On holes number 1, 6, 8, and 9 the water hazards are lateral.

Japanese grass is typical of the courses in this region because it best suits the climate. On average, the greens measure 400 square meters. Most of them are level; only those on holes 1, 2, and 7 are not level.

On this course expect heat, a lot of heat. It is complicated and implacable: don't even think of trying to attack it.

HOLE	PAR	HAND	🟦	🟥	HOLE	PAR	HAND	🟦	🟥
1	3	16	146	136	10	3	16	146	136
2	4	10	309	269	11	4	10	309	269
3	4	2	371	311	12	4	2	371	311
4	3	14	184	155	13	3	14	184	155
5	5	4	530	403	14	5	4	530	403
6	5	12	475	411	15	5	12	475	411
7	4	8	328	278	16	4	8	328	278
8	4	6	390	340	17	4	6	390	340
9	3	18	155	155	18	3	18	155	155
IN	35		2888	2458	OUT	35		2888	2458
					TOTAL	70		5776	4916
					RATING			68.4	66.6

RUITOQUE GOLF COUNTRY CLUB

Address: Piedecuesta Avenue, km 7, Bucaramanga
Altitude: 1330 meters above sea level
Average temperature: 18 °C
Yards: 6601
Holes: 18, par-71
Designer: Golden Bear (1997), actually Nicklaus Design
Bucaramanga population: 550 000

When you play this course, remember that it is not advisable to attack it, as the penalties for mistakes are stiff. You must be precise at the tee off and be careful with the second shot; the greens are very well guarded by all sorts of threats. They are uneven, difficult to read and have a lot of slopes: it is hard to calculate the putt.

The course has a modern design, lies on a high rocky terrain, and is surrounded by sheer cliffs. In the absence of trees to provide a sensation of depth and with the presence of so many hollows and crags, the player becomes confused and it is difficult for him to calculate distances in this setting.

Hole number 2 is a marvel: the view of the town of Piedecuesta at your feet is incredible Your shot will have to fly more than two hundred yards in the air to cross the ravine; the green is protected by three bunkers.

From hole number 17, you are afforded a privileged vista of the cordillera. The hole is a par-4 of 408 yards and outs to the left with the cliff. The fairway narrows from the tee to the landing area, which obliges you to drive precisely: to shoot toward the left side is certain perdition. The green is long, narrow and crooked. Two bunkers to the left may protect your ball; it is recommendable to play toward the center of the green and not attack the flag, especially when it is to the left.

All holes on this course have five tees and are planted in Bermuda 419. The majority are rounded and oval.

The width of the fairways varies a great deal. Some are very narrow and the invasive rough tightens them to 16 yards. Others are as wide as 80 yards.

Four large lakes cross six of the course's holes.

The seventy-three bunkers are deep and straightforward and the loose white sand allows for your best explosive shots. Hole number 16 has the only grass bunker.

Almost all greens are planted in tifton dwarf: they are elevated and uneven, and measure on average between 580-600 square meters. They are all guarded by deep bunkers.

There are not many trees in this dry, desert-like region, whose most characteristic vegetation is scrub grass. *Jalapo* trees, the only variety you will see, are native to the region Although the typical bird of the region is the partridge, you also find cardinals, canaries, *arroceros*, blue jays and the white eagles that fish in the lakes.

"Playing golf in the clouds," is the sensation the course transmits on the frequent occasions when the morning mist settles over the greens and tees.

HOLE	PAR	HAND Women	HAND Men	⬛	🟦	⬜	🟨	🟥	HOLE	PAR	HAND Women	HAND Men	⬛	🟦	⬜	🟨	🟥
1	3	14	14	185	178	155	147	138	10	4	13	13	388	369	348	312	274
2	4	12	12	350	320	305	263	240	11	3	17	17	176	169	157	140	125
3	4	8	8	410	378	345	261	247	12	4	7	3	462	445	420	381	322
4	3	16	16	196	184	166	142	129	13	4	11	11	319	307	294	270	232
5	4	4	4	412	382	361	332	301	14	3	15	15	184	167	146	138	104
6	4	10	10	396	377	353	320	296	15	4	5	1	445	430	402	351	260
7	5	2	2	480	469	444	424	418	16	5	1	5	530	523	500	487	419
8	3	18	18	169	150	148	130	114	17	4	7	3	408	382	365	320	285
9	5	6	6	539	494	475	447	419	18	5	9	9	552	531	509	461	393
IN	36			3137	2932	2752	2466	2302	OUT	36			3464	3320	3141	2860	2414
									TOTAL	71			6601	6252	5893	5326	4716
									RATING				73.1	71.6	70.1	67.2	69.5

CLUB CAMPESTRE DE BUCARAMANGA

Address: Cañaveral-Floridablanca Highway, km 5
Altitude: 960 meters above sea level
Average temperature: 23 °C
Yards: 6346
Holes: 18, par-72
Designer: Mark Mahannah
Bucaramanga population: 550 000

This short, frank course demands strategy and sound execution in every shot. On the hard surface of the fairways and greens the ball bounces a lot, a factor that should form part of your strategy. Also remember that the strong crosscut of the grass on the greens will influence your putting.

Located in the valley of the river Frío, between the mesa of Bucaramanga and the mesa of Ruitoque, this course makes use of the natural topography of the terrain. The presence of so many mature trees shows that the designer valued them and decided to incorporate them into the layout of the course.

Hole number 11, a par-4 of 405 yards, has a dogleg to the left and is nicknamed the "frog hole" for the big frog, sculpted in stone, that appears at the 120 yard marker, next to an enormous *caracolí* tree. Further on, a brook diagonally crosses the area before the green. Therefore your only shot is to chip the ball onto the green; if not, the ball will certainly fall into the brook. The green has three bunkers around it.

The tee on number 16 is elevated and her green stands even higher: the fairway is occupied by a lake which enters at around the 90-100 yard marker; in the center of the lake there is a *ceiba* tree which adorns and complicates the hole.

Most of the tees are elevated, rectangular platforms: they are planted in sweet grass or *trenza*.

The level fairways are uniform and traditionally designed, and have an average width of 30-35 yards. They are planted in a combination of Bermuda 419, Japanese and *remolino*.

The roughs, planted in *remolino*, *trenza*, *san agustín*, and Japanese grass, are jammed with large trees of hard leaves that are densely placed, which make them a major obstacle. Among them you will see: acacias, *caracolíes*, almonds, *guayacanes*, *gallineros*, *pomarrosos brasileros*, *panacos*, *búcaros*, *tulipanes*, and *ceibas*. They attract many birds, such as parrots, woodpeckers, canaries, hummingbirds, and blue jays, and you will also see many squirrels and iguanas.

Frontal lakes affect play on nine holes of the course. Only three – 1, 2, and 18 – are without them. On the rest of the course you will find two brooks and ten lakes.

The greens, sown with Bermuda 238, are surrounded by Japanese grass. They measure 280 square meters, on average, and nearly all are level, with a strong crosscut, generally in the direction of the water.

HOLE	PAR	HAND	🟦	⬜	🟥	HOLE	PAR	HAND	🟦	⬜	🟥
1	4	5	398	385	371	10	3	18	177	171	152
2	3	17	174	151	144	11	4	2	405	366	317
3	4	15	346	338	322	12	4	14	334	334	274
4	5	1	589	551	530	13	5	6	481	470	450
5	4	13	306	292	257	14	4	12	307	295	283
6	4	7	392	376	334	15	4	10	367	356	309
7	3	9	206	197	254	16	3	8	188	146	138
8	5	3	525	496	393	17	5	4	480	465	449
9	4	11	333	321	289	18	4	16	341	330	291
IN	36		3266	3107	2794	OUT	36		3080	3107	2663
						TOTAL	72		6346	6040	457

RATING	72.1	70.9	72.9

WESTERN ZONE

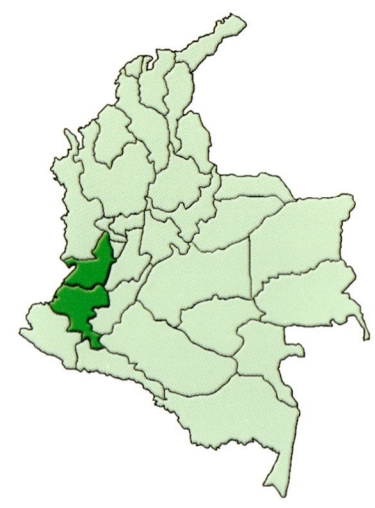

This zone occupies an enviable position. It is comprised of the Departments of Valle de Cauca and Cauca. The variety of topography, climate and vegetation provides it with a strong economic base composed of agro-industry and tourism. Nature finds it most majestic expression here, which is reflected in the beauty of its golf courses.

This region encompasses mangrove swamps, the lowland jungles of the Pacific coast, mist forests and high Andean moors. It also has dry, nearly desert-like regions, which form a contrast with its tropical rainforests and many rivers and lakes.

In pre-Colombian times, this region was rich in indigenous cultures, as may seen from its archaeological monuments, like the ruins of Tierradentro which it shares with the central zone. In its museums you will see the fabulous works in gold and ceramics that they created. At the present time the Guambiano and Paéz indigenous groups still live in parts of the Department of Cauca, where they play an important role in its cultural, political and social life.

The Department of Cauca Valley is one of the most industrialized parts of Colombia and is responsible for the production of foodstuffs, beverages, pharmaceuticals, textiles and books and magazines. Cali, its beautiful capital, is known, not only in Colombia but throughout the world, as the home of Salsa. One of the principal events of the year are the end-of-the year festivities, which combine bullfighting with the tropical music and dancing of the "Feria de la Caña" (Sugarcane Festival). This event is complemented by the cultural activities that take place at the "Mono Núñez" Festival of Andean Music and the Latin American Festival of Folk Dance.

Popayán, the seignorial capital of the Department of Cauca, is one of the most beautiful cities in Colombia and a jewel of colonial architecture. It has a wealth of historical and ecclesiastical monuments. Its famous Easter Week celebrations conserve a tradition that goes back to colonial times and has been zealously conserved by its inhabitants.

The four golf courses that are found in Cali reflect the diversity of the region: the Club Campestre, Club Farallones, Club Shalom and, very near the city, on the road to Popayán in the town of Santander de Quilichao, the Club Los Andes, which attracts many tourists. Further south, in Popayán, you will find that city's Club Campestre.

Playing on any of these courses is an unforgettable experience. You will meet up with open, hospitable, friendly, sincere people and find courses where Nature is boundless. The great expanses of land, rich in vegetation, will make you feel that are you are playing golf in the promised land.

Los Andes Golf Club

CLUB CAMPESTRE POPAYÁN

Address: Old Road to Cauca
Altitude: 1760 meters above sea level
Avereage temperature: 19 ℃
Yards: 2801
Holes: 9, par-34
Designer: Juan Zambrano, first 6 holes (1982). Jaime and Rafael Villegas, reform and expansion to 9 holes (1992)
Popayán population: 230 000

   Surrounded by the mountains of the central and western cordilleras of the Colombian Andes, in the beautiful Valley of Pubenza, you will encounter the golf course of the Club Campestre of Popayán.

   If you play this course, you will have to strategically place the ball on tee-off; the fairways are very narrow and the greens require great precision.

   Hole number 8, a par-5 of 585 yards, is the longest and most complicated hole of the course. The tee is in the lowest part of the hole. The right side is delimited by an out; and parallel to it, enormous trees border the left side; hence, the first 280 yards of the fairway are very tight. The frontal lake, located 210 yards from the green, is accompanied by a grove of guadua bamboo on the right, whose large, leafy branches reach nearly to the center of the fairway. These branches may easily deflect the ball into the lake: thus, it is best to play for the left of the fairway. Past the lake, the fairway begins to climb towards the green, which is raised 30 feet above it. The green is long and narrow and protected by a bunker in front and an out on the right and at the back.

   The tees are rectangular and planted in kikuyo. The fairways are narrow and uneven, with constant rises and dips that reflect the topography of the terrain.

   The sixteen bunkers, most of them deep and surrounding the greens, are filled with a white cliff sand.

   The roughs, cut to nearly the same level as the fairway, are easy to play. However, the great variety of trees in them, which serve to delineate the fairways, make life difficult for the golfer. Stands of eucalyptus, *fresno*, willow, walnut, *chocho*, *veranera*, *arrayán*, *tulipan*, palm, *zapote*, guadua, orange, lemon and mango form a thick wood that complicates play and requires precision and skill from the golfer.

   A large marsh, and seven little lakes, placed strategically around the course, are an added challenge. The greens are not very irregular and measure on average 350 square meters.

   The upper reaches of the course provide another atmosphere. From the tee of number 9 you may enjoy a panoramic view of the whole course. The imposing cordilleras give you the feeling that you are approaching all that is sacred in life. A refreshing waterfall that descends from a rugged rock towards the green of the eighth will bring you back to earth and remind you that you have to keep playing the game.

HOLE	PAR	HAND	■	□	■	HOLE	PAR	HAND	■	□	■
1	3	15	181	172	161	10	3	16	181	172	161
2	4	9	378	355	301	11	4	10	378	355	301
3	3	7	193	183	172	12	3	8	193	183	172
4	5	3	500	480	440	13	5	4	500	480	440
5	3	5	235	230	135	14	3	6	235	230	135
6	4	13	269	262	238	15	4	14	269	262	238
7	3	17	121	121	116	16	3	18	121	121	116
8	5	1	584	543	487	17	5	2	584	543	487
9	4	11	340	327	258	18	4	12	340	327	258
IN	**34**		**2801**	**2673**	**2308**	**OUT**	**34**		**2801**	**2673**	**2308**
						TOTAL	**68**		**5602**	**5346**	**616**
						RATING			**68.5**	**64.2**	**65.9**

FARALLONES CLUB CAMPESTRE

Address: El Banco Avenue, 127st street, Alférez Real estate
Altitude: 1100 meters above sea level
Average temperature: 25 ºC
Yards: 7402
Holes: 18, par-73
Designer: Fernando Gamboa. Jaime and Rafael Villegas, construction first 9 holes (1972). Luis Herrera, next 9 holes (1984). Subsequent modifications approved by Fernando Gamboa and executed by Luis Herrera.
Cali population: 2 270 000

Be prepared to play on an immense golf course in a landscape of high mountains, volcanic peaks, and a lush riverside vegetation alongside the Pance River. The club lives up to its name, which might be roughly translated as "The Cliffs"

The main characteristic of this course is its length: 7402 yards. Not surprisingly, hole number 11 is the only par-6 on any course in Colombia.

Ample areas of garden are interwoven into a course that is appropriately designed and full of daring challenges. The range of greens harmoniously blends into the colorful clothing of the golfers and is complemented by the subtle hues of heliconia, *achira*, ginger and bougainvillaea flowers.

Hole number 11 is perfect for long hitters. If you are one of these, you will reach the green in three shots. You will then have a good chance of making an eagle.

The sixth, a par-3 of 89 yards, is beautiful. The green is protected by a lake and a surrounding bunker. The fairway has a level, slightly rolling, terrain which is perfectly framed by pines, araucarias and cypresses.

The tees are rectangular and, like the fairways, are planted in Bermuda 419: The fairways are 25 yards wide, on average.

The roughs are planted in *trenza* mixed with a wide variety of native vegetation. Some of the plants are flowering, ornamental varieties, while others produce such fruits as mangos, oranges, lemons, guavas and *guanabanas*, which are complemented by immense trees which are harmoniously shared by lizards and squirrels.

There are forty-two bunkers, mostly level, which surround their greens tenaciously; furthermore you will find fifteen cross-bunkers in other critical places, which complicate an already challenging course.

Turtles, *peyares*, eagles, hawks, stone-curlews, parrots, *toches*, egrets, geese, and ducks fly overhead or light on the twenty three small lakes on this course.

The greens, planted in Bermuda 328, measure on average 355 square meters and are very fast. Half of the greens are level while the other half are rolling.

Blessed by the landscape of the western cordillera and the majestic cliffs at the entrance to Cali, this course is designed for your enjoyment. Great golf and a beautiful landscape: what more can you ask for?

HOLE	PAR	HAND	🟦	⬜	🚩	🟥	HOLE	PAR	HAND	🟦	⬜	🚩	🟥
1	4	10	433	412	393	340	10	4	5	472	432	422	412
2	5	4	562	505	496	481	11	6	7	710	677	602	571
3	3	18	172	164	164	160	12	3	15	214	196	188	181
4	4	12	412	400	398	340	13	4	9	411	396	340	294
5	4	14	410	390	375	335	14	4	11	404	390	380	342
6	3	16	189	170	156	144	15	4	1	452	426	378	365
7	4	6	427	396	370	320	16	4	13	384	364	344	312
8	5	2	550	530	505	453	17	3	17	185	170	155	140
9	4	8	420	400	385	355	18	5	3	595	580	525	495
IN	36		3575	3367	3242	2928	OUT	37		3827	3631	3334	3112
							TOTAL	73		7402	6998	6576	6040

RATING		74.4	72.2		73.2

ASOCIACIÓN CAMPESTRE SHALOM

Address: La María-Pance Avenue
Altitude: 1006 meters above sea level
Average temperature: 23 °C
Yards: 3142
Holes: 9, par-36
Designer: Raúl Posse and Salvador Pinzón (1963)
Cali population: 2 270 000

On this course you will be obliged to use short irons all the time. It is a place that requires exactitude, because of the traditional design that incorporates a high degree of difficulty. The fairways, narrow and level, are surrounded by thick stands of mango trees, which often interfere with the game. The greens are easy to land on and the ball does not run excessively.

From the tee of hole number 5, a par-3 of 189 yards, the Pance River runs along the entire left side of hole. At 80 yards the river forks and one arm crosses the fairway. From that point onwards the hole is flanked by its banks and its water eventually surrounds the green. The crosswinds make this hole even more difficult.

The biggest challenge of this course is hole number 9: it is long and difficult, especially the shot to the green, which is elevated above the fairway and has an out at the back.

Hole number 6, a par-3 of 208 yards, has a tree in the middle of the fairway, while a brook runs to the left and a lake stands on the right, making it a tricky but beautiful hole. Two bunkers surround the green.

An automatic sprinkler system waters the entire course from the tees to the greens. The drainage system relies on the natural topography of the course and is highly efficient.

This course has many water hazards: twenty-one lakes and eight brooks that tcross the course twelve times; there are also twenty-eight sand hazards.

Squirrels, *peyares*, parrots, herons, ducks, woodpeckers, *titiribíes*, blackbirds, *viudas*, *tijeretas* and *cucaracheros* are some of the birds and animals you will find here, along with the *tilapias* and *sabaletas* that swim in its lakes and streams.

It is easy to fall into the bunkers, filled with white sand and not very deep, that surround most of the greens. It is customary to use a putter to get out.

In the roughs you will find mango, rubber, avocado, *tulipan*, palm, tangerine, orange, *madrono*, lemon, breadfruit and *mamoncillo* trees, along with an abundance of orchids, and bougainvillaea.

The fairways and roughs are planted in *trenza*. The grass on the areas before the green is crosscut, which makes a precise use of the club difficult. You must be very alert when making your approach shot. The greens are fast and planted in Bermuda.

Don't be surprised if you find billy goats along the course: they are one of the eccentricities of this club.

HOLE	PAR	HAND	🟦	⬜	🟥	HOLE	PAR	HAND	🟦	⬜	🟥
1	5	7	476	449	406	10	5	7	476	449	406
2	4	13	299	293	287	11	4	13	299	293	287
3	4	3	383	374	284	12	4	3	383	374	284
4	5	1	486	469	396	13	5	1	486	469	396
5	3	17	189	135	125	14	3	17	189	135	125
6	3	15	208	203	186	15	3	15	208	203	186
7	4	11	319	315	312	16	4	11	319	315	312
8	4	9	366	365	342	17	4	9	366	365	342
9	4	5	416	395	331	18	4	5	416	395	331
IN	**36**		**3142**	**2989**	**2670**	**OUT**	**36**		**3142**	**2989**	**2670**
						TOTAL	**72**		**6284**	**5978**	**5340**

RATING		72.1	70.9	

CLUB CAMPESTRE DE CALI

Address: 5th Street Avenue 100
Altitude: 1000 meters above sea level
Average temperature: 25 ºC
Yards: 6902
Holes: 18, par-71
Designer: Howard Watson, Canadian Golf
Landscaping Ltd. (1956)
Cali population: 2 270 000

A typical example of mid-20th century design, this course is austere. It is completely integrated into the natural topography, which is not to say that it lacks variety. The design and layout of the holes are surprisingly diverse.

Hole 7, a par-4 of 405 yards, climbs gradually from the tee to the green along a straight line. This hole is probably the most difficult of the course. The first shot demands precision, due in part to the limited space – 25 yards in width – of the landing area. If your shot goes well you will then be given an equally precarious second shot: up to the green which stands four meters above the fairway. It is protected on the right side by a deep bunker and on the left and at the back, by a severely inclined rough. This hole's deceptive green poses two problems: first club selection and second, the risk of falling into the bunker.

Its traditionally-designed tees are planted in *trenza*; the fairways are narrow, measuring 25-30 yards. They have gentle undulations and are planted in Bermuda 328. The roughs are also sown with *trenza*. This strong, dark grass forms a contrast with the fairways, both appearance and in the way it allows the player to hit the ball. The course has 78 shallow bunkers filled with river sand and the majority are oval in shape.

Twelve lakes on this course, with their connecting canals, constitute the water hazards.

The roughs show the rich flora that characterizes the natural beauty of this course and provides shelter for the animals who live in or visit it. They includes iguanas, *peyares*, *guacharacas*, ducks, and *guatines* and other birds. You will also find six different types of palms and a wealth of mangos, cedars, *samanes*, *ceibas*, *caracolies*, *cachimbos*, *madronos*, bamboo, *guayacanes*, avocados, *guanabanas*, *tulipanes*, *icacos*, *caimos, nísperos* and *carboneros*. These stands of trees delineate the holes and their foliage obliges you to play for the middle of the fairway.

The greens are planted in Bermuda and tifton dwarf: the greens vary – some are slightly undulated, others have severe slopes, others are relatively level and still others have two levels. Generally, the greens are narrow.

In short, this course offers a pleasant blend of water, vegetation and wildlife, in a design that suits the game and your experience as a player.

HOLE	PAR	HAND	🟦	⬜	🟥	HOLE	PAR	HAND	🟦	⬜	🟥
1	4	13	389	374	371	10	3	16	222	194	188
2	5	1	560	520	482	11	4	10	376	335	288
3	4	11	403	367	336	12	4	12	372	343	298
4	3	15	208	175	138	13	5	2	502	475	440
5	4	5	446	423	388	14	3	18	195	195	176
6	3	17	156	156	145	15	4	4	417	395	335
7	4	9	405	344	315	16	4	8	399	385	329
8	5	3	599	552	492	17	4	14	353	340	300
9	4	7	461	421	361	18	4	6	439	395	361
IN	36		3627	3332	3028	OUT	35		3215	3057	2715
						TOTAL	71		6902	6389	6743

RATING	🟦 73.3	⬜ 70.6	🟥 73.1

LOS ANDES GOLF CLUB

Address: Cali-Popayán Road, km 35
Altitude: 950 meters above sea level
Average temperature: 27-30 °C
Yards : 7030
Holes: 18, par-72
Designer: Rafael Villegas and Jaime Villegas (1990)
Cali population: 2 270 000

If you have heard the expression "lakes are psychologically difficult," then on this course you will be sorely reminded of its truth. On this course you will find water, lots of water, and her lakes pose the true challenge. Almost all of them are strategically designed and placed to penalize mistakes. To play on Los Andes Golf Club is to assume an exacting and precise challenge.

Hole number 1 is a true test of your modesty. This 379 yards par-4 doglegs to the left and has a lake on the left that runs along its entire length to the green. From the tee, situated on an island, you can see the entire hole. The long hitter will be tempted to drive straight for the green, but unless you are sure of a shot of at least three hundred yards, don't even consider it, since your ball can easily find its way into a lake. Therefore the best way to land the ball is to the right of the fairway, keeping clearly in mind the out which also threatens on the right. The second shot presents its own challenge: the green, which is surrounded by two bunkers and has a lake in front on the left, seems insurmountable. The lesson to be learnt here, at hole 1, is indispensable to the knowledge that will enable you to deal with the remaining holes: don't use an attack strategy, ever.

The fairways are planted in Bermuda 328, while the roughs are planted in a *trenza* which demands a precise stroke, for there are tall, full-branched trees that threaten any wobble. You will see *samanes*, *carboneros*, *tulipanes*, *mandarins*, lemons, eucalyptuses, pines, *grosellos*, *guamos*, *ceibas*, *veraneras*, and *crotos*, all part of the rich exuberance of tropical vegetation. The 49 bunkers are filled with white river sand.

The greens, all planted in Bermuda 328, are level, easy to land on and a bit slow. They measure, on average, 500 square meters.

You will see and hear a lot of birds, such as *peyares*, *titiríbíes*, blackbirds, *viudas*, *tijeretas* and *cucaracheros*, which adds to the pleasure of the game.

When you finish your round, linger at hole 9 to experience the show that Nature offers at sunset and watch the black and white heron taking its ritual rest on the hole's tall tree.

HOLE	PAR	HAND	🟦	⬜	🟥	HOLE	PAR	HAND	🟦	⬜	🟥
1	4	7	379	343	292	10	5	2	572	496	418
2	3	15	179	153	127	11	4	14	389	341	304
3	4	5	429	386	362	12	4	6	428	374	342
4	5	1	595	505	492	13	3	16	185	167	142
5	3	17	206	173	153	14	5	4	552	483	452
6	4	9	406	347	318	15	4	12	355	329	291
7	4	13	373	353	337	16	4	10	413	359	326
8	5	3	570	521	485	17	3	18	185	143	138
9	4	11	418	406	352	18	4	8	396	377	362
IN	36		3555	3157	2918	OUT	36		3475	3069	2781
						TOTAL	72		7030	6252	5699
						RATING			73.0	71.3	73.1

"Golf is a science, a lifelong study in which you may exhaust yourself but never the subject. It is a struggle, a tourney that requires and demands courage, skill, strategy and self-mastery. It tests the steadiness, measures the honor and reveals the character of the person who plays it. It offers a man the chance to display his game and the gentleman, his dignity"

If, on the terrain which is entrusted to you, you manage to create a golf course that not only respects and highlights the natural setting but is also a diverting, challenging and memorable one, you will have fulfilled your task as a course designer.

JACK NICKLAUS

The challenge of creating a competitive and technically suitable course is not the only one a designer faces. He is responsible for the destiny of an inspiring setting with sources of water that should be exploited in the best possible way for the benefit of the game and the terrain, a local vegetation that should be respected and a sacred place of infinite possibilities. These factors turn the designing of golf courses into a sublimely creative activity.

BORIS SOKOLOFF

You will never have two holes that are exactly the same in the world. The characteristics of each course prevent it: topography, type of terrain, altitude, climate, water, vegetation. In Colombia the truth of this affirmation is infinitely strengthened by the intrinsic variety of the country. That is why each design should be a product of the designer's creativity and his capacity to take advantage of the given conditions.

RAFAEL VILLEGAS

In the design of golf courses I have always kept in mind one of the best suggestions that are found in Dr. A. Mackenzie's book, "Golf Architecture in 1920": "You have to combine and harmonize the design of the course with nature in such a way that no one will notice the hand of man when it is finsihed".

FERNANDO GAMBOA

We use our vision to reveal and sculpt the course that corresponds to each site, so that golfers may enjoy the challenges and wonders of the game.

ROBERT TRENT JONES, JR.

The course must be a permanent source of pleasure for the greatest possible number of players: it must be friendly to the average player and demanding for the expert one.

SCOTT MILLER

Los Andes Golf Club
Page. 276, *Asociación Campestre Shalom*
Page. 277, *Club Campestre de Cali*
Page. 278, *Mesa de Yeguas Country Club*
Page. 279, *Corporación Club Lagos del Caujaral*
Page. 280, *Club Campestre de Cali*